Islamic Banking

Principles, Practices and Performance

Islamic Banking

Principles, Practices and Performance

By

A. Abdul Raheem

Associate Professor,
Department of Economics,
The New College (Autonomous), Chennai

New Century Publications
New Delhi, India

NEW CENTURY PUBLICATIONS
4800/24, Bharat Ram Road,
Ansari Road, Daryaganj,
New Delhi - 110 002 (India)

Tel.: 011-2324 7798, 4358 7398, 6539 6605
Fax: 011-4101 7798
E-mail: indiatax@vsnl.com • info@newcenturypublications.com
www.newcenturypublications.com

Editorial office:
LG-7, Aakarshan Bhawan,
4754-57/23, Ansari Road, Daryaganj,
New Delhi - 110 002

Tel.: 011-4356 0919

First Published: **July 2013**

ISBN: **978-81-7708-357-6**

Published by New Century Publications and printed at Salasar Imaging Systems, New Delhi.

Designs: Patch Creative Unit, New Delhi.

PRINTED IN INDIA

About the Book

Commercial banks and other financial institutions are an integral part of present economies. Individuals as well as public and private institutions can hardly operate without the institution of banking. Modern banking operations are primarily interest-centric. Banks receive money and lend it on interest. This is prohibited in Islam. Since interest permeates all the operations of the banking system, the whole banking system is repugnant to Muslims.

Islamic banking—as an alternative to the Western capitalist banking system—prohibits any kind of speculation, interest, and immoral investments (e.g. casinos). Islamic banks have to make a profit. They do this by buying assets on behalf of the customer, who has to repay the *loan* and a fee for using the asset. When the *loan* is paid off, the asset's ownership is transferred to the borrower. The advantage of this arrangement is that the bank shares not only the profit but the risk as well. For this reason, it gets the opportunity to have a close look at the potential borrowers.

This book deals with conceptual, theoretical and empirical framework of Islamic banking system. It also provides a performance review of Islamic banks in global perspective. More importantly, it explains and examines the practices of Islamic banking in India, focusing on issues and constraints. Finally, it suggests the need for establishment of Islamic banks in India and areas of further research in the subject.

Author's Profile

Dr. A. Abdul Raheem is presently Associate Professor, Department of Economics, The New College (Autonomous), Chennai. He did his M.Phil. and Ph.D. from Annamalai University, Tamil Nadu. He has contributed numerous research articles in reputed national and international journals and published 4 books. He successfully completed two research projects funded by University Grants Commission (UGC), New Delhi.

Dr. Raheem is recipient of distinguished scholar in economics award from Southern India Chamber of Commerce and Industry. His areas of research interest include micro finance, Islamic banking, rural development, and women empowerment.

Contents

1.1 Islamic Banking System
1.2 Need for an Islamic Banking System
1.3 Concept of Islamic Banking
1.4 Major Channels of an Islamic Bank
    1.4.1 Mudharabah (A Method of Trust
           Financing)
    1.4.2 Musharakah (Which Covers Equity
           Participation and Decreased
           Participation)
    1.4.3 Murabaha (Cost plus Profit Margin
           in Trade or Other Financing)
1.5 Functions and Dimensions of an Islamic
    Bank
1.6 Conventional Banks versus Islamic Banks
    1.6.1 Similarities
    1.6.2 Differences
1.7 Structure of Islamic Banks
    1.7.1 Banking Operations
    1.7.2 Investment and Financing
    1.7.3 Legal and *Fiqhi* Jurisprudence
    1.7.4 Financial Control
    1.7.5 Administration (including Training
           and O&M)
    1.7.6 Planning, Research and
           Development
    1.7.7 Control
    1.7.8 Social Activities and Community
           Services

Contents

Preface

Islamic banks are banking institutions that provide the banking services within the boundaries of Islamic principles. Islamic banks cannot offer a loan to earn interest or discount a commercial bill or grant any drawing facilities. Further, Islamic banks are not allowed to deal in swaps of different currencies because of the involvement of the interest between the two currencies that are exchanged on forward basis. The Islamic banking system draws a clear distinction between services and financing activities.

According to Islamic principles, usury is forbidden and the *Mudharabah* system is commonly used as a vehicle for investment especially for those people who cannot do the job themselves, like the soldiers, orphans or government officials. Scholars in different sectors and school of thought recognized *Al-Mudharabah* contract as an accepted deal. In later stage, development of Muslim society witnessed a third party who could work as a mediatory between the providers of the capital and the beneficiaries. The third party will be a trustworthy person who used to take the money from those who were looking for investment. The new thing is that the trusted person did not work by himself but he used to give such money to a qualified person who could do the job. The profit of the trusted person is derived from the difference between the percentage he agrees to take from the owner of the capital (say 50 percent of the realized profit) and the percentage that he can impose on the user of the borrowed money (say 60 percent). The trusted person in his role as a mediator will play the same role as it is played now by the modern banks, i.e. taking the deposit to use the same to others. Under this system of single and double *Mudharabah* contracts, a long lasting civilization did arise under the umbrella of Islam.

For millions of Muslims, banks are institutions to be avoided. Their Islamic beliefs prevent them from the dealings that involve usury or interest (riba). Yet, Muslims need banking services for many purposes as much as anyone else needs, and to finance new business ventures, to buy a house, to buy a car, to facilitate capital investment, to undertake trading activities or to offer a safe place for savings. For Muslims who are not averse to legitimate profit as Islam encourages people to use money in Islamically legitimate ventures, not just to keep their funds idle.

Islamic banking, based on the Qur'anic prohibition of charging interest, has moved from a theoretical concept to embracing more than 300 Islamic financial institutions, which operate worldwide in about 75 countries. Patrons of Islamic banking and finance are not confined to Muslim countries but are also spreading over Europe, the United States, the Far East, South Asia and the Middle East. Assets of Islamic banks worldwide are estimated to be more than US$ 265 billion and of financial investments above US$ 400 billion. Islamic bank deposits are estimated at over US$ 202 billion worldwide with a growth rate between 10 and 20 percent. The best known feature of Islamic banking is the prohibition of interest. The *Qur'an* forbids charging of *riba* (an Arabic term having a wider meaning than Interest) on money lent. It is important to understand certain principles of Islam that undermine Islamic finance.

The *Shari'ah* disallows *riba* and there is now a general consensus among Muslim economists that *riba* is not restricted to usury but encompasses interest as well. Today the world economic system which is based on interest has resulted in wealth in the hand of select few individuals and widening the gap between rich and poor. In contrast, Islam encourages circulation of wealth and regards its role as important in world economy similar to the flow of blood in human body. Just as clotting of blood paralyzes human body, the concentration of wealth amongst few individuals paralyses economy. The fact is that today 10 richest men in the world have more wealth than combined assets of 48 poorest countries of the world. Millions are malnourished, lack access to safe water, cannot read or write. In short, the quality of life has decayed and the graph continues to go down.

Economic justice requires a viable economic system supported by an efficient banking system. Interest-based banking has proved to be inefficient as it fails to equitably distribute wealth amongst all section which is necessary for the benefit of mankind. On the other hand, Islamic banking is efficient and ensures equitable distribution of wealth thus laying foundation for an inflation-free economy and socially responsible banking. Last few years have witnessed a dramatic increase in Islamic banking across the world. At least two hundred Islamic banks and financial institutions have been set up. According to a research report, the growth rate of these institutions is 15 percent per annum. Many multinational banks have opened Islamic banking windows or subsidiary of Islamic banking. On the *Shari'ah* side there are a number of scholars on Shari'ah boards of Islamic banks who have compiled Fatwas, resolutions and articles on various issues of Islamic banking and finance. There are at least two comprehensive reports on Islamic banking system produced by Islamic Ideological Council (1980) and the Commission for Islamization of Economy (1992).

Therefore, Islamic banking is not a utopian idea. There is a need to educate and train the bankers in the Islamic economic and banking system. Without having a deep understanding of the principles of Islamic banking, it is difficult to offer products and services that conform to the true spirit of Islamic shariah.

I take this opportunity to place on record my deep sense of respect and gratitude to my beloved parents and teachers for their love, affection and support. I record my special thanks to Dr. A.K. Ramalingam, Formerly Professor, Department of Economics, Annamalai University for his encouragement and moral support. I am immensely grateful to Janab Asraf Sahib, Honorary Secretary and Correspondent, The New College for his help and guidance. Thanks are also due to Dr. Abdul Maliq, Principal, The New

College; Dr. Syed Fazlul Huq, Head of the Department of Economics, The New College; Dr. M.H. Zawahirullah, Formerly Professor of Commerce, Islamiah College, Vaniyambadi and Dr. S. Thangaraj, Professor and Head of Department of Economics, University of Madras, for their co-operation and constant encouragement.

Chennai   **A. Abdul Raheem**
June 2013

1

Introduction

1.1 Islamic Banking System

Islamic banks are banking institutions that provide the banking services within the boundaries of Islamic principles. As any other bank, an Islamic bank can operate a current account, savings account, sell or buy different currencies on spot basis, open a letter of credit advice and confirm or issue a letter of guarantee, etc. What the Islamic bank cannot do is the paying or charging of any kind of interest under any name or form. Therefore, Islamic banks cannot offer a loan against interest or discount a commercial bill or grant any drawing facilities. Further, Islamic banks are not allowed to deal in swaps of different currencies because of the involvement of the interest between the two currencies that are exchanged on forward basis. [1]

The Islamic banking system draws a clear distinction between services and financing activities. As for the banking services, history gives us numerous examples regarding the development of these services whether it was practiced by organized banking institutions as we have it in our present time, or handled through different methods as the old Sumerians or Babylonians used to do it in their Sacred Temples centuries before Christ. [2]

The Islamic religion which spread over most of the old known countries in the 7th and 8th century contains the guidelines as to what is permitted to be done and what is prohibited. Islam, as the Muslims believe, is the last ring in the chain of God's mission to the human beings. Since the early days of Islam, the prohibition of usury was one of the basics of the Muslim society. Before Islam, the heathen Arabs used to lend and borrow on usurious basis in a similar manner as the

Jews who were living in Arab peninsula. Those Arabs also knew a unique kind of partnership where one party provides the capital and the other does the work on the basis of participation in the profit.

According to Islamic principles, usury is not allowed and the *Mudharabah* system is commonly used as a vehicle for investment, especially for those people who cannot do the job themselves—like soldiers, orphans or government officials. Scholars in the different sectors and schools of thought recognized *Al-Mudharabah* contract as an accepted deal. In later stages, development of Muslim society witnessed a third party who could work as a mediatory between the providers of the capital and the workers. The third party was a trustworthy person who used to take the money from those who were looking for investment. The new thing was that the trusted person did not work by himself but he used to give such money to a qualified person who could do the job. The profit of the trusted person is derived from the difference between the percentage he agrees to take from the owner of the capital (say 50 percent of the realized profit) and the percentage that he can impose on the user of that money (say 60 percent, for example).

The trusted person in his role as a mediator played the same role as it is played now by the modern banks, i.e., taking the deposit, to be lent to others. Under this system of single and double *Mudharabah* contracts, a long lasting civilization did arise under the umbrella of Islam. At that time, trade was controlled by Muslims in the international markets at Baghdad and Alexandria, which decided the prices of the different commodities; like it is determined now by London, New York or the Zurich market.

The reason for this is the system itself. In the Islamic system, the capital owner should search for a partner who is usually an ordinary worker with a good name. This worker becomes a partner who gradually turns to be self-employed or even an employer if his business can expand. While in the modern banking system where money can be lent only to those who can provide collateral, one can see that the wealth becomes automatically monopolized and concentrated in the hands of a limited class. The majority becomes a working class and the middle class also vanishes.

An expert engineer or genius doctor cannot find any value to his human ability as long as his pocket is empty. Such a person should look for employment. But in an Islamic system, the picture is entirely different. There is no place for borrowing money on the basis of being wealthy because borrowing is not an allowed as a vehicle for investment. If the capital owner is willing to invest his money, he should search for a partner or work with his money himself. By doing so, the system paves the way for eliminating gradually, the number of workers who would be turned partners.

This is a self-mobilized system that has kept the different Muslim societies for hundreds of years enjoying a cordial and peaceful life compared to other societies which have adopted the usurious economical system. As for the banking services, it may surprise to many researchers to know that the Islamic civilization did witness the birth of numerous banking activities including safe deposits, transfers, exchange, drafts and issuance of cheques (which is in fact an Arabic word taken from "*suck*" that means "a written order"). [3]

The first cheque in history was not that written order which was drawn by an English goldsmith in the year 1675 in London; but the first real cheque was that which was drawn by the Prince of Alepo in the Tenth century (Saifudawlah Al-Hamdani who was on a visit to Baghdad). The story of that cheque was that this Prince wanted to give a present to some people who did not know him. He wrote an order directed to the Exchanger of Baghdad and when they went to encash the money, they knew that the cheque was signed by the Prince whose signature was verified by the Exchanger. Knowing that Baghdad was a different state from Alepo, one should expect that a clearing system was in existence by that time.

This incidence of Saifudawlah is not the only case like the English Londoner in the year 1675, but there were many cases of cheques drawn on different exchangers. One such unique incident is registered in the Encyclopaedia of Literatures. It is mentioned that a poet named Fatha (who lived in around the tenth century) received a cheque which he failed to encash and returned it to the drawer with two lines of poems that recorded the first returned cheque case. He said to the drawer, "If your drafts are only a piece of paper which is not cashable, then I would be ready to write you a cheque of million Dinars as far as it is not payable". [4]

As for the exchange deals it was known as an exchange between different currencies (golden Dinar against Dirhams of silver).

The Prophet (PBUH) of Islam explained that the governing rate in this case should be the prevailing rate of the day of the deal. Forward exchange on swap basis was not allowed due to the fact that in every exchange deal, different currencies should be delivered immediately.

It is amazing for our present understanding to know that the Prophet (PBUH) of Islam did mention that such a delay in the case of exchange was considered to be usury.

This fact was revealed only in our times after the development of the foreign exchange markets. It was noticed that the difference in the interest rate would be represented in the forward exchange offered price. [5]

In Al-Basra city (in Iraq), the development of business of banking reached its peak in the tenth century when the Persian traveller Naser Khasro passed by the city at that time. He gave a detailed description of its market procedures. It was supposed that every person who entered the market should hand over all his cash money to the market exchanger who would give him certain papers to be used as cash. These papers were generally accepted. When such person wanted to leave the market, he would find the exchanger ready to give him the balance left with him. All these selected incidents in the field of banking activities which had developed under the umbrella of the Islamic civilization prove to us many things, as follows:

1. That Islam as a religion does not contradict in principle with the business of banking.
2. The prohibition of usury did not form a constraint in the development of a suitable vehicle for providing the finance and practicing the investment of funds according to the needs of society at that time.
3. The Islamic principles unlike the other previous heavenly religion such as Christianity and Judaism, do not accept usury in general. Besides, Islam as the last mission gave a practical solution for the achievement of the socio-economic role in a balanced manner between capital and labour.
4. As a result, one should not look at the contemporary Islamic banking movement as an isolated step that is separated from the glamorous history of the past Islamic civilization.
5. Each nation has its role to play. Despite the present weak situation of the nations of Muslims, there is still a base for better guidance that would serve the needs of our modern society.
6. The principles of Islam are a belief to a Muslim but it can be a relief solution to a non-Muslim also. As one can take the Indian wisdom without being an Indian, the non-Muslims can benefit from the guidance of Islam without being followers of the Islamic religion; as Islam is a belief the very spirit of which is dead against any imposition by force.

1.2 Need for an Islamic Banking System

For millions of Muslims, banks are institutions to be avoided. Their Islamic beliefs prevent them from the dealings that involve usury or interest (Riba). Yet, Muslims need banking services for many purposes much as anyone else needs—to finance new business ventures, to buy a house, to buy a car, to facilitate capital investment, to undertake trading activities, and to offer a safe place for savings—for Muslims are not averse to legitimate profit as Islam encourages people to use money in Islamically legitimate ventures, not just to keep their funds idle. However, more than 1,400 years after the Prophet, can Muslims find room for the principles of their religion, in this fast moving world?

The answer comes with the fact that a global network of interest free banks popularly known as 'Islamic banks' has started to take shape, based on the principles of Islamic finance laid down in the *Qur'an* and the Prophet's Traditions, 14 centuries ago. Islamic banking, based on the *Qur'anic* prohibition of charging interest, has moved from a theoretical concept to embracing more than 300 Islamic banks and financial institutions, which operate worldwide in some 38 countries. [6] Patrons of Islamic banking and finance are not confined to Muslim countries but are spread over Europe, the United States, the Far East, South Asia and the Middle East. Assets of Islamic banks worldwide are estimated at more than US$ 265 billion and financial investments above US$ 400 billion. Islamic bank deposits are estimated at over US$ 202 billion worldwide with average growth between 10 and 20 percent. [7]

The best known feature of Islamic banking is the prohibition on interest. The *Qur'an* forbids the charging of *Riba* (an Arabic term having a wider meaning than interest) on money lent. It is important to understand certain principles of Islam that underpin Islamic finance. The *Shari'ah* consists of the Qur'anic commands as laid down in the *Holy Qur'an* and the words and deeds of the Prophet Muhammad. The *Shari'ah* disallows *Riba* and there is now a general consensus among Muslim economists that *Riba* is not restricted to usury but encompasses interest as well. The *Qur'an* is clear about the prohibition of *Riba*, which is sometimes defined as excessive interest. "O You who believe! Fear Allah and give up that remains of your demand for usury, if you are indeed believers." Muslim scholars have accepted the word *Riba* to mean any fixed or guaranteed interest payment on cash advances or on deposits. Several *Qur'anic* passages expressly admonish the faithful to shun interest. [8]

In a Muslim society, the need for Islamic banking is very important. Any Muslim who knows Arabic could not help thinking of the clear meaning of usury and its results when he reads what is written in the *Qur'an*. When a person or a group of people act passively in dealing with their money, the social effect would not be limited to that specific person or group of people only, but it would affect the different sectors in the society. If money was kept at home or deposited in a current account, the national economy would be suffering from the unnecessary increase of the money supply.

For a true Muslim, the need for a suitable banking system is very important. Because money in Islam has a special consideration—it is not allowed to hoard money or spend it without any reason. There is a social responsibility for the use of money and there is also an annual percentage of 2.5 on savings to be spent for charitable purposes according to the categories explained in the *Qur'an*. [9] Between these two ends, the existence of an Islamic bank becomes a must. When money is deposited, there shall be no hoarding. The investment of such deposits would give the answer for the social responsibility and the profits could help the owners to pay their *Zakat* (social charity tax). From this point, one scan conclude that if there was no banking system in the world, there should be an invention of such a banking system which would satisfy the needs of the believers in Islam.

1.3 Concept of Islamic Banking

The prefix 'Islamic' before 'Bank' is only a kind of distinction as we say—the housing bank or an industrial bank—but this distinction is meant to be directed to the way of doing the business rather than the sector itself. The business of banks can be classified into three categories:
- Banking services,

- Exchange dealings, and
- Credit trade, i.e., borrowing and lending; or in other words taking deposits and loans to be invested in lending.

As for the banking services, there is not much difference between an Islamic bank and a traditional one. The letter of credit and letter of guarantee, the transfer of money, the collections and the safe deposit are provided in the same manner. The only difference comes when there is a rise of a lending-borrowing relation as in the case of the payment of the bill of exchange drawn under a letter of credit without having a sufficient balance to cover the overdraft. In such a case, there is no place for charging interest.

As for the commission, it can be charged by an Islamic bank and as far as it is related to any kind of a service—except the service of lending or borrowing money. A commission for advising a letter of credit, amendment or confirmation etc. is all accepted. Commission in the Islamic terminology is known as "*Ajr*" which means the compensation for doing a work or providing a service. As far as the work or the service is acceptable, the commission paid for it, is legitimate. As for the exchange dealings, an Islamic bank can buy and sell different currencies including gold and silver as coin or as bullion. The only consideration that should be observed in this matter is related to the conditions of the deal itself.

If the exchanged currencies were of the same kind, i.e., US Dollar for US Dollar or Pound Sterling for Pound Sterling, the two exchanged currencies should be equal in value and the delivery of the two currencies should be at once without any delay. But in case of the exchange of different currencies, as Pound Sterling for US Dollar, the exchange deal could be done according to the spot rate of exchange with an immediate delivery of the two exchanged currencies. The swap sale and purchases deal in foreign currencies is not permitted in spite of the rumours that some Islamic banks were doing this kind of transaction in currencies, gold and silver. The saying of the Prophet (PBUH) of Islam is very clear about this point of usury in sales. The sale of gold for silver (which covers any exchange dealings involving two different currencies) is considered to be usury unless the two currencies were exchanged immediately.

The Islamic banks can do the business without being involved in the forward swaps of the exchange dealings. When we move to borrowing and lending activities, the matters become different. Any extra repayment rather than the original principle in any lending-borrowing relation is considered to be usury. Usury in Islam is considered to be one of the big sins. In Islam, there is no difference between usury as an excessive interest or the so-called legal interest itself. Therefore, depositors who in fact are a lender to the bank cannot be allowed to take interest in the Islamic measures; but he can be an investor. The percentage of profit must not be offered the same conditions applied to other investors by receiving a portion of the profit that comes out of the pool of the investment portfolio managed by the bank. The relation with the user of funds is not a borrowing-lending relation; but it has a different type of contractual arrangement.

1.4 Major Channels of an Islamic Bank

The main major channels used by an Islamic bank in providing its finance are the following.

1.4.1 Mudharabah (A Method of Trust Financing): Advances given by one party; say the Islamic bank which shall provide the necessary funds, fully or partially, for financing a specific activity mostly in trade that is administered by the other partner on a profit-sharing basis. In case of loss without any negligence or violation by the partner to the terms and conditions of the contract, the capital owner bears the loss and the working partner loses the expected profit. This type of financial contractual relation covers the need for a working capital in the trading activity where capital is needed on a transitory basis or bridge-over finance. There should be a systematic arrangement for liquidation of the assets in order that the two parties can make an actual cash-base of the financial position and the distribution of the realized profit. [10]

1.4.2 Musharakah (Which Covers Equity Participation and Decreased Participation): *Musharakah* is a method of participation. In case of equity, there is nothing new; but in case of the decreased participation, the idea looks different. This case of funds participates, fully or partially, in a profitable project, on the basis of a mutual agreement with the other partner that the bank shall be a transitory partner. The profits realized in the project which might be financed one hundred percent by the bank can be divided into three portions which are not necessary to be equal. For example, the arrangement can be as follows:

- 30 percent of the actual realized net income is given to the bank as a profit.
- 20 percent is given to the other partner as a part of his portion of the profit.
- 50 percent is kept in an escrow account for the purpose of setting-off the rights of the bank when the accumulated income becomes equal to the bank's original participation in the project.

It is obvious that this kind of decreased participation represents a special design whereby the bank can open the doors for professionals and others to become owners of a specific profitable project by giving a little effort of thinking and good management. This contract is an idea that has developed as a specific type of *Al-Mudharabah* in which the capital is not used in trade activity as it was in the past days. The capital here in this case is used as a means of real development whereby the partner becomes the owner of the project that he is managing, not merely a trader on profit basis.

1.4.3 Murabaha (Cost plus Profit Margin in Trade or Other Financing): This contract is a unique contractual relation whereby the bank purchases, upon the request of an applicant, the things needed by the applicant on the basis of an open undertaking by him to re-purchase what he ordered to be bought at a profit as it is agreed upon in advance. This type of financing method is helpful in many cases whereby the *Mudaraba* or *Musharakah* does not work. For example, there cannot be a place for *Mudharabah* or *Musharakah* in the case of financing the personal needs or self-used equipment such as private cars or radar equipment.

It is also applicable in the case of buying and selling raw material such as copper or aluminium to be used by General Motors in the car industry. Here, Al-Murabaha comes as a perfect solution. The bank can buy the raw material in cash and sell it back to the end-user on deferred payment basis, according to the time needed for manufacturing or marketing the product. This type of double contractual relation was not commonly used in the past days of the Islamic civilization in spite of the fact that it was mentioned in the famous book of a leading luminary of the Islamic jurisprudence. The possibility of this type of financial mediatory is found in an old book of Imam Shafi who lived in Egypt around 9th century A.D.

The importance of this *Murabaha* contract is related to the size of the finance involved in this activity. More than 80 percent of the Islamic banking activities are using the *Murabaha* contracts despite some objection where some writers try to say that such a contract should not be a binding or it is rather a cosmetic structure and not a real trade. It is a genuine contract as far as it is used for a real need either for trading or using things bought and sold. The osmotic deals which are used deliberately to go around usury such as buying a commodity from A by B on deferred payment, then selling the same commodity by B to A on cash basis, is forbidden. It is obvious in this case that the commodity was a mere vehicle used as coverage for borrowing. For a Muslim who believes in God's knowledge of every single move, it is difficult to think that he can cheat his creator. God knows the open and the hidden thoughts of a human being. [11]

In addition to these main methods of financing, there are

many other means such as *Salam* contract (pre-paid purchase) in which the bank can buy the further production, agricultural or manufactured, through an advance payment for the full price at a discounted rate. Also there is the leasing arrangement in the form of hire-purchase system. Besides, the Islamic system is open for any new arrangement that can satisfy the public needs if there was no violation to the basic principles of Islam, mainly no usury, monopoly or exploitation. When that big power and influence of the capital is controlled, the doors could be opened for the social development and the Islamic banking system could play its role in a peaceful way.

1.5 Functions and Dimensions of an Islamic Bank

Islamic banking or preferably called "Partnership/Profit and Loss Sharing banking" is an economic and financial system based upon and operated according to the jurisprudence and the rules of the economic and social order of Islam. The founders of most of the Islamic banks put the set of rules to govern their activities in the form of articles of association; statues and by-laws and sometimes under different headings such as objectives; scope of work etc. The common features and main functions of most of the Islamic banks are:

1. Establishing, developing and operating a financial and banking institution conforming to *Shari'ah.*
2. Helping in establishing and developing capital markets according to *Shari'ah* and promoting *Takaful* (insurance) business.
3. Supporting studies and research on Islamic economics, finance and banking.
4. Promoting business and trade relations among Muslim countries and encouraging trade financing and export-oriented products as a substitute to imports.
5. Financing projects and long-term investments.
6. Equity participation and shareholding either in already established and successful companies, or in new ones in

various sectors of the economy.

7. Financing, managing and up-lifting troubled companies with good potentials and sell them afterwards (Islamic leverage by-out).

8. Financing small-scale industries and encouraging artisans and skilled people.

9. Issuing *Mudharabah* bonds and investment certificates to finance public enterprises and to participate in building the infrastructure of the economy along the development plans of the country.

10. Contributing to social projects and activities.

11. Extending traditional banking services on commission basis.

12. Mobilizing deposits and other funds.

As realized from this wide range of objectives, scope of work and instruments used to realize these objectives, scholars have outlined the main dimensions of this type of institutions as follows:

A. Development Dimension: Has deep roots in the production of various sectors of the economy and has a wide social impact that focuses along the objectives of government development plans.

B. Universal Dimension: Combining the activities of commercial banks, investment banks (merchant) and social banks. It is in a word, an economic institution rather than a financial one.

C. Ownership: Equity dimension through direct ownership of companies or projects and equity financing.

D. Direct Pro-active Dimension: Not merely being a financial mediator. This is extended to be a catalyst for a positive social and economic change.

E. Social Dimension: Restricting its role not only to investment and financing and subsequently maximizing the profit of shareholders but also balancing the interests of all parties of "social contract" i.e. shareholders, depositors, users of funds, beneficiaries, investors, general public using the services of the bank, and the society at large.

F. Legal/*Shari'ah* Dimension: Exclusive and restrictive functions according to *Shari'ah* jurisprudence. [12]

1.6 Conventional Banks versus Islamic Banks

Before we discuss the managerial and practical aspects of Islamic banks, it may be useful to compare these banks with the conventional banks in broad terms to identify similarities and differences.

1.6.1 Similarities:

- Both are governed by the general rules of the regulatory authority covering establishment, control and general operations.
- Both operate within the context of professional efficiency, cost effectiveness and cost-benefit.
- Both are directed towards useful employment of resources for the society (with different emphasis, of course).
- Both are usually established as shareholding companies.

1.6.2 Differences:

- Islamic banks have a different moral basis, i.e. jurisprudence (*Shari'ah*).
- Consequently, targets, objectives and mode of operations are different.
- Islamic bank is a universal "comprehensive" bank; whereas in conventional framework, there is a commercial, investment, merchant or a specialized bank.
- Structures of assets and liabilities i.e. sources and uses of funds are different and consequently the earnings and expense structures are different.
- Because of the *Shari'ah* restrictions and the prohibition of usury, the detailed relationship to the regulatory authority is different.
- Target customers are partly different.

1.7 Structure of Islamic Banks

The organizational philosophy and consequently the

managerial concepts and structures are reflections and practical applications of the overall objectives and ultimate targets of a bank. This is why, the organization of an Islamic bank, reflecting its peculiar characteristics, is by definition not similar to a conventional bank. There is no one prototype of an organizational structure for an Islamic bank, because of the following:

- Different legal and administrative regulations in different locations and regions.
- Professional and practical requirements in a given banking society.
- The possible size and complexity of operations and market.

Despite these sources of diversity, it is, however possible and desirable to describe the main features of the organization structure based on the main functions of Islamic banks. The organization structure will be based on the following main divisions:

- Banking operations,
- Investment and financing,
- Legal and *Fiqhi* jurisprudence,
- Financial control,
- Administration (including organization and training),
- Planning, research and development,
- Control, follow up and audit, and
- Social activities and community services.

Highlighted below are the main functions of these divisions.

1.7.1 Banking Operations: The main point of departure here is the types of deposits and investment accounts as they are required to receive different treatments based on profit/loss as compared to the interest-based deposits of conventional banks.

1.7.2 Investment and Financing: This includes short-term, medium and long-term financing, diminishing/decreasing or permanent partnership, equity participation and the like.

Here, we notice the diversity of products and the need for extensive experience in all fields and especially financial analysis, economic and social feasibility studies and most importantly, opportunity/project identification. Checking customers and partners accounts and finances also play an essential role here.

1.7.3 Legal and *Fiqhi* Jurisprudence: The implication of medium to long-term financing; project financing and equity participation puts tremendous pressure and responsibility on the shoulders of the legal department towards documentation and legal structures of partnerships or deals. The *Shari'ah* jurist is the main vehicle to evaluate, approve contract documents and supervise all operations of the bank in conformity with its objectives and ultimately with principles of Islamic laws. It is the absolute responsibility of the legal or any related department to observe and maintain these rules and regulations. It is as well, the due obligation of the legal/*Shari'ah* advisor to monitor and check transactions on random basis. All types of new contracts have to be reviewed and agreed upon by him. A general statement of the *Shari'ah*/legal advisor should be issued to the general shareholders meeting in connection with the annual audited accounts of the bank, certifying conformity to *Shari'ah* rules and accepted *Shari'ah* interpretations and practices. This, of course, implies special manpower requirement with the needed qualification and experience.

1.7.4 Financial Control: This function does not differ from any conventional bank, except in the following two main directions:

- The Islamic bank is a universal bank with equity participation in subsidiaries, sister companies and the like. This means that the final shape of the balance sheet should be like that of a holding type company to reflect the true picture of the whole set of operations and involvements;
- The chart of accounts and details of accounting principles applied are different from those of a conventional bank

which has to be observed, maintained and developed. It requires exceptional qualities of personnel as well.

1.7.5 Administration (Including Training and O & M): As stated earlier, since the organizational set up is different, the criterion of selection and the details of qualification of staff is therefore also quite different from a conventional bank. Though standard rules apply here as well, as for training, this aspect relates to types and quality of staff needed to perform the peculiar kind of functions which require initial and on-going training not only in the disciplines of Islamic banking and the mission oriented jobs, but also the continuous development of products and instruments based on *Shari'ah* rules. Quality of the chief executive and board members makes no exception. In fact, there is a huge moral and professional responsibility on the boards of such banks.

1.7.6 Planning, Research and Development: Planning function is principally the same as in conventional banks with two exceptions:

- It includes planning of complex and sophisticated product mix and activities.
- It includes planning for the bank; including subsidiaries and (to a certain extent) associated companies and projects as a holding structure.
  Business ethics of Islam should be taken into consideration. Research and development covers many areas including:
- Collecting economic research and statistics.
- Studying trends and developments to identify prospective opportunities in sectors, projects or markets.
- Marketing research on products/customers (investors, partners and depositors).
- Developing services and conventional products, as well as new products in conformity with *Shari'ah* rules in coordination with similar banks in a dynamic and continuous way.

1.7.7 Control: This includes internal audit, follow up and evaluation of projects and equity participation, and the external audit.

A. Internal audit: It does not differ from the traditional elements applicable in any bank. The only difference being in the details of operations which have to be considered while auditing. The extra qualification of staff in *Shari'ah* disciplines is required.

B. Follow up and Evaluation: Since the bank has this multiple function of financing, long-term/partnership investment and equity shareholding, it requires special emphasis and certainly special qualification of staff and system in:

- Follow up and evaluation plans for projects; and
- Institutional control measures to monitor and guide the activities of subsidiaries and sister companies to safeguard the investors' interest.

C. External Audit: This function by and large does not differ from the generally accepted rules. Some differences, however, may appear in respect of the following:

- Qualification of the external auditor in this type of banking and its implications.
- The kind of statements he makes by the end of the year taking into consideration not only to safeguard the interest of stockholders, but also the depositors being effective partners with the bank and affected directly by the performance of the management.
- Conformity with the accepted rules of Islamic accounting principles and practices as adopted by similar banks.
- A close liaison should be developed between the external auditors (representing the shareholders) and the legal/*Shari'ah* advisors (representing the jurisprudence). It is important to note that the legal/*Shari'ah* Advisor is sometimes appointed directly at the shareholders' meeting.

1.7.8 Social Activities and Community Services: Apart from the financing and investing activities and extending banking services, the bank should be actively involved in the

social activities and community services, such as:
- Establishing and/or managing social funds.
- Contributing to social activities in various forms such as gifts, contributions, promotion of business and social ethics, social research etc.
- Collecting and managing *Zakat*, *Hajj* and *Umrah* funds.
- Encouraging labour-intensive projects and enterprises, individual initiatives of entrepreneurs and promoting venture-capital investments; thus relieving the burdens of employment from the shoulders of the public sector.
- Extending benevolent loans for the general public or for charity without return. [13]

1.8 Islamic Bank: Some Critical Issues

After this brief summary of the main functions, it seems appropriate to concentrate on some basic issues which have to be dealt with at some length because of their significant impact on the success of Islamic banks, i.e. marketing, partnership, balances, accounting rules and standards, and relations with the regulatory authority.

1.8.1 Marketing: Marketing is not just one activity that a business undertakes. Instead, it is an organizational philosophy that influences and directs all the operations of a bank. Indeed, it constitutes the bank's orientation towards its business. This is what is defined as a marketing philosophy. To be effective, the bank should develop the marketing concept, i.e. the frame of mind and the basis for decision-making and a guide for effectively managing the resources. Marketing by definition is managing a change or more specifically, initiating a change that is within the control of the bank. In one word, marketing is defined as:
- A bank's philosophy;
- A practical concept;
- A process of change and exchange; and
- A means of success.

The position of a bank towards marketing is one of the

following:
- Marketing is essential and necessary.
- Marketing is necessary but non-essential.
- Marketing is non-essential but expedient.

When applying the definition and the concept to Islamic banks, we realize that marketing is to be considered as an integral element within the mental framework of an Islamic bank in spite of the fact that it is based on a different set of rules such as:
- Different objectives not only for maximization of profit, rather for promoting interest for the economy/individual.
- Different tools.
- Different products.
- Different sets of media contents.
- Different abilities of marketing personnel.

The concept of change and exchange in the behaviour of customers (depositors, shareholders, entrepreneurs and fund-users) is an essential tool for marketing, which is closely related to the term *Dawah* which is mission orientation. This behaviour of the bank management towards marketing falls into the first category mentioned above i.e. essential and necessary. Therefore, this function should be given a special attention and effort. At the same time, it entails the greatest challenge for the bank to effect the change desired. The process should start with creating awareness and end with definite positive results.

1.8.2 Partnership Balances: The function and operation of the Islamic banks is to identify following parties that could be related to a "socio-economic contract" because of the nature of relation and dependency amongst them. They are, shareholders, staff, investors and depositors.
- The partnership between the shareholders and the management of the bank.
- Employees/employers partnership relation.
- The degree of efficiency and productivity and cutting of expenses determines amongst others, the ultimate gains for

the stockholders.

Some scholars suggest a margin of percent of gross profit to cover the personnel and general expenses as a maximum. Deriving from this suggestion, the ratio of proceeds assigned for fund collectors of *Zakat* fixed by the doctrine at 1/8th.

- The higher the expenses, the higher the percentage of the bank's share from the profits of depositors to cover the expenses and a margin for the stockholders as dividend.
- The partnership relation between the depositors of an investment funds and the bank as fund manager. The higher the percentage of the bank from investment proceeds, the lower would be the return of depositors and vice-versa.
- The partnership-relation between the bank as fund providers and its clients as the fund users. The percentage of profit/loss–cost of funds affects the return to the bank and consequently the depositors.

The higher the share of profit (cost of funds), the higher the return to the shareholders (the bank) and the depositors and vice-versa (economic and inflation impacts are worth considering).

From the above illustration, we anticipate the striking balance required between all parties in a fair and just manner for themselves and for the economic community.

Control measures and safeguards should be observed to serve the correct balance of interests.

1.8.3 Financial Standards and Reporting: It has been accepted that the accounting standards, rules and procedures are reflections and translation of a given economic enterprise and its nature, based on certain values of the community and its degree of sophistication. Islamic banks are not the exception; therefore they should have a set of rules and standards that reflect truly their nature and types of operations; as good as the structure of assets and liabilities reflect the nature of these banks. Experience of Islamic banks demonstrate the need for setting the Islamic Accounting

Standards to meet the requirements of modern banking practices based on the deep and rich sources of knowledge of Islamic economics and finance.

The existing Financial Reporting Standards, which have been developed in harmony with the International Accounting Standards (IASs), have not been able to address accounting issues within Islamic banking operations adequately. Fundamental differences in underlying principles, along with the distinctive nature of Islamic financial practices, have rendered many facets of conventional accounting standards irrelevant to Islamic banking. Hence, the existing Financial Reporting Standards and prevailing IASs are useful in providing a structural framework for reporting, but they are inadequate to accommodate *Shari'ah* precepts, which form the basis of all Islamic transactions.

The Accounting and Auditing Organisation for Islamic Financial Institutions (AAOIFI), an accounting and auditing standards setting body in Bahrain, has been active in developing and promoting Islamic accounting, auditing, and *Shari'ah* standards. The standards issued by AAOIFI have been instrumental in codifying accounting and auditing norms and rules. They also have helped to focus energies and elevate the level of discourse among bankers, policy-makers, and others, about the imperative of standardisation and harmonisation for the Islamic financial services industry at large. [14]

Since 1991, when the Islamic banking and finance industry itself decided that the existing international standards were inadequate to cater to its needs, AAOIFI have come a long way to being recognised as the main standard-setting organisation. AAOIFI have now issued 56 standards on accounting, auditing, governance, ethical, and *Shari'ah* standards, including a statement on capital adequacy. Over the years, AAOIFI has taken significant steps to encourage the application and enforcement of its standards throughout the world. AAOIFI have done so by producing high-quality standards that are internationally recognised and have made particular efforts to ensure that their standard setting process constitutes strong cooperation amongst interested parties.

Recently, the General Assembly of AAOIFI approved the increase of its technical board from 15 to 20 members. This decision will further boost the adoption and implementation of AAOIFI's standards where they are either mandatory or used as a guideline by the regulators in jurisdictions such as Bahrain, Sudan, Jordan, Malaysia, Qatar, Saudi Arabia, UAE and Lebanon. Most recently, Syria signed an agreement to mandate and adopt AAOIFI's standards.

It is only through international recognition and consistent application of these standards will the Islamic banking and finance industry realise the full benefits of accurate and transparent financial reporting, and fulfil its mission of bringing credible solutions to the masses. As the main avenue for the interface between market players and regulators, AAOIFI membership continues to expand, which now stands at around 200 members from 45 countries (as in 2013). This steady progress is a reflection of the confidence placed in AAOIFI as the leading representative of the industry.

1.8.4 Relationship with Regulatory Authority: Most of the regulatory authorities control functions that are operating more or less within the context of the "Anglo-American" model of regulations and supervision. The emerging new Islamic banks presented a problem and a challenge to those authorities, because of the restrictions and the unique nature of the new banks. The basis on which the Islamic banks are operating in various countries is quite different in form and content:

- Some are operating within the context of existing banking regulations. They are basically accommodating their operations within the legal boundaries of the countries, while making their operations according to *Shari'ah* rules (e.g., Islamic banks in US and UK);
- Some are operating within the context of existing

regulations, but with a wider flexibility and recognition of their different nature by the regulating authority— cooperation developed useful modus operandi with the respective authorities (e.g., Islamic banks in Bahrain, Mauritania, Tunis, Singapore, and Bangladesh etc.);

- Some are working within the general context of existing regulations, but have their own status and laws separately used and agreed upon by the authorities. This arrangement enables these banks to work freely to a great extent (e.g., some banks in Egypt, Jordan Islamic Bank, Islamic banks in Malaysia);

- Others are working under the umbrella of a decree or special law regulating the whole issue of "Islamic Banking and Investment", with limited relationship to regulatory authority (e.g., Islamic banks in Turkey and the Philippines);

- Some are operating under the general umbrella of the whole "Islamized system" (e.g., Islamic banks in Iran, Pakistan and Sudan).

It is quite difficult to analyze all models and situations; however, looking back to different experiences in the last decade, the idea of issuing a special comprehensive "package" for such banks may be most appropriate and desirable.

The International Association of Islamic Banks initiated under the auspices of the Organization of Islamic Conference (OIC), organises regular meeting at experts' level between experts of Islamic banks and representatives of central banks in the concerned countries to discuss issues of common interest.

Experts of central banks and Islamic banks have been meeting for almost twenty five years now. Both parties have showed equal interest and care to ensure the success of the new experiment of Islamic banks. The well organized procedures of the meetings, the fruitful discussions based on in-depth studies, gave Islamic banks a unique chance to present their problems and aspirations. The relationship of an

Islamic bank to a regulatory authority is usually organized by legislation, administrative measures and morale persuasion to serve the purposes of both sides in different aspects.

1.8.5 Aspects of Relationship: Typical main areas cover the following:

- Ownership and controlling rights.
- Licensing and branching.
- Capital and reserves.
- Seeking financial assistance from central banks.
- Cash reserves and liquidity requirements.
- Financing and investment operations and their economic and monetary impact.
- Tax structure on various modes of operation.
- Holding equity, property, title of goods etc.
- Inspection.
- Cost of funds, profit return to depositors and dividends to shareholders.
- Supervising interest of depositors.
- Information.

If the basis of foundation and operations is clear, less would be the problems in future. However, even in cases of highest order of regulations and degree of transparency in the relation, there is no alternative to the continuous discussions for beneficial understanding and success. This factor is a predominant contributor to the success of an Islamic bank. Therefore, it could be concluded that the establishment of Islamic banks in a number of countries signifies the challenging and pioneering ideas and actions of founders to demonstrate a practical solution for modern banking operations in conformity with the *Shari'ah* and responding to the aspirations and needs of millions of customers. Beyond that, it is a practical manifestation of the Islamic social and economic doctrines and interpretations. An effective Islamic bank requires, amongst others, the following to secure its success.

- A clear and basic foundation as a legitimate and ultimate

source of authority with a clear mandate and acceptance.
- A comprehensive statute and articles of association with a clear vision in conformity with its basic principles.
- Detailed by-laws and manual of operations and procedures.
- An organizational concept and a structure, that is effective, reflective and dynamic.
- Qualified staff, mission-oriented and challenge-facing with continuous training and knowledge.
- A chart of accounts and accounting standards as a true translation and reflection of its nature of operations.
- Control functions, based on checks and balances to safeguard interests of all parties concerned.
- A "package" or set of rules and guidelines to regulate the relationship with the regulatory authority, and a sound working relationship based on trust and cooperation.
- Liaison and intensive relationship to similar banks benefiting from their experience and exchange of ideas and views.

1.8.6 Interest-free Commercial Banking: Banks are an essential component of the present day world. Individuals as well as public and private institutions can hardly operate without the institute of banking. Commercial banking as we find it today, evolved over time and has become a stable institution, with principles and procedures that are well understood, accepted and practiced throughout the world. Modern banking operations are primarily based on interest. Banks receive money on interest and lend money on interest. This is prohibited in Islam. Since it permeates all the operations of the banking system, the whole banking system is repugnant to the Muslims. To remove the element of interest from commercial banking, we must first understand the precise role it plays in the system. Then we can examine the effects of removing it from the system and see if the resulting system is still viable.

In the context of modern banking, the depositor is the

actual lender and that so long as he does not demand and/or receive any interest from the borrower (of course, through the bank), the whole business of commercial banking is free of interest. For the lender lends his money free of interest, the borrower receives his loan free of interest, and the bank–the intermediary–receives only a fee for its services. Once this vital point is understood, the main objection to lending in conventional commercial banking becomes devoid of any basis. The other services offered by a commercial bank are free of any element of interest. Hence, freeing the conventional commercial banking of interest is very simple. Once this is done, the time-tested techniques of conventional commercial banking can be used without any further ado. The changes that need be made are thus more conceptual in nature and involve very little modifications in practical procedures. Customer service extends beyond spot transaction. It is more than effectively meeting the customer needs or handling of their grievances. [15]

Customer service would be better if employees develop the desired attitude and motivation and develop their capabilities in the direction of effective customer service. Customer service is in fact the perception of a customer of the services he gets from his bank. The human perception changes from individual to individual and within an individual from time to time. [16] This change in perception of a customer of the service he gets makes the job of satisfying him at all point of time more challenging. [17] It is, therefore, necessary for banks to continuously assess and reassess how customers perceive the services, what are the new and emerging customer expectations and how they can be satisfied on an ongoing basis. "Customer service is not merely the fulfilment of Government's guidelines or mechanical adherence to the time frames of services. It is a philosophy, an attitude of professional commitment which believes in the ultimate satisfaction of a customer's want". [18]

The major element of service that a bank can offer to a

customer is the feeling that he/she is not just another number in computer, but a person in whom the bank takes a personal interest and with whom he/she can interface when problems arise. The computer and modern methods of analysis can be helpful in this regard. But in communicating the results, a little bit of human touch is essential. Furthermore, the frustration caused by impersonal services will allow the bank to give it a human face. [19] 'Customer satisfaction', through face to face interactions, looks for ways to make customers feel special. This special feeling is created through pleasant surprises; unique action or qualitative approach to service. [20] The essence of service excellence concentrates on listening, empowerment, innovation and making customers and employee's a part of the action. Service excellence focuses on making the service, the products and the surroundings more convenient, easier, neater and unique.

Service excellence builds on excitement, relationships and trust. While a quality service approach uses some of these elements, they form the heart of service excellence. The service organizations like banks play an important role in marketing various banking services to customer. Banks, basically work on the goodwill of the customers. [21] The best way of servicing and prospering in the competitive environment is by providing prompt, relevant and efficient customer service at reasonable cost. The common bank customer now-a-days, is not fully satisfied by the services rendered by the banks. The level of satisfaction in the customer service offered by the banks is generally related to their counter services and time taken in providing some of the essential service facilities like collection of cheques issue of statement of accounts, e-banking facilities.

The employees as well as banks must realize that good service does not mean merely treating the customer politely and putting through their transactions with expedition. [22] It basically implies ascertaining and assisting the customer's requirements, needs and expectation and then initiating a management process to fulfil and integrate these with the organization's goals and objects. In a manufacturing industry, the nature of the product handled is tangible and permanent; in service-oriented organizations, it is intangible and perishable and therefore, service is hypersensitive. [23]

Customers are won and retained by correctly identifying the value they are seeking and then providing it as complete as possible. Competitive value is a matter of optimizing the balance between effectiveness and efficiency. The successful organization is more effective at understanding the customers and winning new ones. Customer care is something a customer is entitled to. It is now widely recognized that if the customer is dissatisfied, the organization has no business to exist. [24] Further, studies have revealed that it is cheaper to retain the existing customer than seeking a new one. It is also true that it is very challenging to retain the existing customer than seeking a new one.

1.8.7 Quality in Service: Quality is a subject that can be viewed from many a different angle. Above all, it is a guideline for providing high level services. By searching for the key elements in the term quality, one should upgrade the level of his services. Quality can be defined quite simply as the degree in which the expectation of customers is met with regards to a service offered. Quality is subjective. Quality in service industries has evolved into two distinct but related fields. The first is service quality and the second is service excellence. These two fields are related as much as the way marketing is related to sales or accounting is related to finance. Just as sales improve with good marketing and finance becomes possible through accounting, customer satisfaction improves when excellence finds its roots, meeting customer needs. These two fields overlap in several areas including listening to the customer, handling complaints and maintaining friendly service.

However, the way each field addresses business customer interaction is distinctly different. Quality service means delivery of promise through the design and execution of repeatable actions. The key to achieving service quality is conforming to standards. Service excellence, on the other hand, addresses to the defects in the present structure. Banking organizations are essentially human enterprises and customer service has therefore, to be necessarily taken care of through the persons working in banks. This has to be done by ensuring that the employees acquire capabilities that contribute to effective customer service, develop the desired attitude towards customers and are motivated to serve the customer better. Employees of banks should have clear knowledge of various schemes of the banks. They should be able to understand the customer requirements and suggest schemes to meet the needs of the customer.

Effective customer service has to be backed by prompt and speedy decision-making process. The concept of accountability has affected decision-making and in turn, the quality of service. Bank executives have changed themselves from leading to galloping procedures, rules and regulations which has resulted into indecisiveness. And this culture has percolated down to the junior most bank employee. The culture has changed from doing right things to doing right–whether it satisfies a customer's want and needs or not is not important. Employees think of their safety first while taking decisions. As global competition in financial services intensifies, service quality is emerging as a new frontier of banking competition. [25]

One reason is the increasing difficulty of competing on the basis of product and price. Many financial products are essentially commodities whose feature can easily be copied, and reliance on price competition is an invitation to steadily declining profit margins.

Customer satisfaction is the key to secure his/her loyalty and generate superior long-term performance. Therefore, banking institutions need to be made more responsive to the needs of the public. In the current context, customer care and customer concern have become much more important. Customers are willing to pay more for higher quality service and competitors are not likely to replicate service dimensions as readily as product features. The service quality challenge becomes even more compelling because of increased role of conventional banks offering Islamic banking services.

As a result, customers who have inclination to do business only with Islamic banks have more opportunity to experience superior service and to compare service levels in different banking institutions. In this trend of competition, banking customers may have a stronger incentive to switch institutions in order to satisfy their rising expectations for service and value. The very nature of service marketing requires that service organizations should devote more attention on offering efficient services to the customers. As the services are invisible, they can gain confidence and goodwill through efficient and prompt customer service only. Therefore, this book emphasis on following main aspects:

- Overview of theoretical framework of Islamic banking system.
- Some conceptual and empirical framework of Islamic banking system.
- An evaluation of global perspectives of Islamic financial institutions/banks.
- Performance of Islamic bank, Bank Islam Malaysia Berhad (BIMB) functioning in Malaysia.
- The practices of Islamic banking system and the issues and constraints in India.

End Notes
1. Khan, Mohsin S. and Abbas Mirakhor (1987), (eds.), Theoretical Studies in Islamic Banking and Finance: Institute for Research and Islamic Studies, Houston.
2. Goitein, S.D. (1967), A Mediterranean Society: University of California Press, Berkley and Los Angeles.
3. Udovitch, Abraham, (1970), Partnership and Profit in Early Islam: Princeton University Press, Princeton, NJ.

4. Duri A. A. (1986), "Baghdad", The Encyclopaedia of Islam, E.S. Brill, Leiden.
5. Khaf, Monzer and Khan, Tariqullah (1992), Principles of Islamic Financing-A Survey, Islamic Research and Training Institute, IDB, Jeddah.
6. Islamic Finance Directory (2004), General Council for Islamic Banks and Financial Institutions, Manama.
7. Figures based on background paper submitted on the Occasion of The International Islamic Finance Forum held from 26-29 September 2005, Istanbul, Turkey.
8. Holy Qur'an, Chapter 2: Verse 275, Chapter 2: Verse 278-281, Chapter 3: Verse 130, Chapter 4:160-161.
9. Holy Qur'an, Chapter 9: Verse 60.
10. Usmani, Taqi Muhammed, (1998), An Introduction to Islamic Finance: Idara Isha'at e Diniyat, New Delhi, p. 47.
11. El-Gamal, Mahmoud Amin (2000), A Basic Guide to Contemporary Islamic Banking and Finance, Rice University, Houston.
12. Ahmad, Ziauddin (1994), Islamic Banking: State of the Art, Islamic Research and Training Institute, IDB, Jeddah.
13. Obaidullah, Mohammed (2005), Islamic Financial Services, King Abdul Aziz University, Islamic Economics Research Centre, Jeddah.
14. Fouad, Al-Omar (2000), Supervision, Regulation and Adaptation of Islamic Banks to the Best Standards: The Way Forward, paper presented to the Conference on Islamic Banking Supervision: AAOIFI, Bahrain, February 18-19.
15. Kamila, B. and Nantel, J. (2000), "A Reliable and Valid Measurement Scale for the Perceived Service Quality of Banks", International Journal of Bank Marketing, 18(2), pp. 84-91.
16. Cronin, J. and Taylor, S. (1994), "SERVPERF versus SERVQUAL: Reconciling Performance-based and Perceptions-minus-expectations Measurement of SQ", Journal of Marketing, Vol. 58, January, pp. 125-131.
17. Yavas, U., Bilgin, Z. and Shemwell, D. (1997), "SQ in the Banking Sector in an Emerging Economy", International Journal of Bank Marketing, 15(6), pp. 217-223.
18. Stafford, M., (1994), "How Customers Perceive SQ", Journal of Retail Banking; 17(2), pp. 29-38.
19. Blanchard, R. and Galloway, R. (1994), "Quality in Retail

Banking" International Journal of Service Industry Management; 5(4), pp. 5-23.

20. Avkiran N. (1994), "Developing an Instrument to Measure Customer Service Quality in Branch Banking", International Journal of Bank Marketing; 12(6), pp. 10-18

21. Buttle, F. (1996), "SERVQUAL: Review, Critique, Research Agenda", European Journal of Marketing, 30(1), pp. 8-32.

22. Gronroos, C. (1984), "A SQ model and its Marketing Implications", European Journal of Marketing, Vol. 18, pp. 36-44.

23. Ennew, C., Reed, G. and Binks, M. (1993), "Importance-Performance Analysis and the Measurement of SQ", European Journal of Marketing, 27(2), pp. 59-70.

24. Mersha T. and Adlakha V., (1992), "Attributes of SQ: The Consumers' Perspective", International Journal of Service Industry Management, 3(3), pp. 55-70.

25. Oliver, R.L. (1993), "A Conceptual Model of SQ and Service Satisfaction: Compatible Goals, Different Concepts", Advances in Services Marketing and Management, Vol. 2, JAI Press, Greenwich, CT, pp. 65-85.

2

Islamic Banking:
Theoretical Framework

2.1 Introduction

The theory of Islamic banking is based essentially on the premise that interest, which is strictly forbidden in Islam, is neither a necessary nor a desirable basis for the conduct of banking operations, and that Islamic teachings provide a better foundation for organizing the working of banks. Muslim economists have pointed out that it is a historical accident that interest has become the king pin of modern banking. The practice of interest has been condemned by foremost thinkers in human history and by all Biblical religions. Aristotle dwelt on the "barren" nature of money and vehemently condemned the institution of interest which he described as "birth of money from money".

Under Judaism, Israelites were forbidden to demand any increase on the principal amount of the sum lent in transactions among themselves though interest could be charged in dealings between Israelites and gentiles. The reason for this distinction, according to many scholars of Judaism, was that there was no law at that time among the gentiles that prohibited the practice of interest, and it was not regarded as unfair that Jews be allowed to recover interest from people who charged interest from them. In Christianity, the reported saying by Christ to "lend freely, hoping nothing thereby" (Luke 6:35) is taken by many commentators as condemnation of interest.

However, the Church gradually changed its doctrine on the subject of interest. In any case, the divorce between religion and mundane affairs accepted by Christian societies after Renaissance opened the door for widespread practice of interest. Among the followers of Islam, the institution of interest has always been regarded as highly ignoble because the Holy *Qur'an* strictly prohibits interest based transactions of all forms.

In the early history of Islam, the injunction relating to prohibition of interest was strictly observed, but with the decline of the hold of religion and spread of Western influence, financial practices based on interest began to permeate the Muslim societies as well. In the period of colonial domination of Muslim countries by Western powers, the interest-based system became solidly entrenched. It is this string of historical circumstances, Muslim scholars argue, which has led to the present-day dominance of interest in financial transactions all over the globe. Had the societies developed in a different fashion and paid greater heed to the injunctions of religion, the development of the financial system would have surely taken a different course, and we could have had in actual operation, an alternative system free of interest but fully meeting the needs of modern society.

Theoretical work on Islamic banking encompasses several aspects related both to the operating procedures of Islamic banks and the possible socio-economic consequences of the adoption of the new system. This chapter deals with the main contributions to the theory of Islamic banking under the following broad heads:
- Concept and models of Islamic banking;
- Viability of Islamic banking; and
- Socio-economic consequences of Islamic banking.

2.2 Models of Islamic Banking

The theoretical work on the concept of Islamic banking has proceeded on the basis that guidance for all institutionalized developments in an Islamic society should be derived from the principles of *Shari'ah*. The form and content of Islamic banking practices have, therefore, to be derived from the teachings of Islam. Scholars in search of a new form of banking which should steer clear of interest noted that though banks did not exist in the early Islamic period, the practice of financial resources of one party being used by another party in the conduct of business, trade or industry was fairly widespread. In the pre-Islamic period, all financial resources were mobilized on the basis of either interest or some sort of profit/loss sharing arrangements.

Islamic banking prohibited all dealings based on interest but allowed the continuance of the system of profit/loss sharing. The two forms of profit/loss sharing which were predominantly in use in the pre-Islamic period are known as *Mudarabah* and *Musharakah*. In mudarabah, one party provides the capital while the other party manages the business. Profit is shared in pre-agreed ratios and loss, if any, unless caused by the negligence or violation of the terms of the agreement, is borne by the provider of capital. In musharakah, partners pool their capital to undertake business.

All providers of capital are entitled to participate in management but are not necessarily required to do so. Profit is distributed among the partners in pre-agreed ratios while loss is borne by each partner strictly in proportion to respective capital contribution. The jurists of the early Islamic period closely examined the features of mudarabah and musharakah as found in the pre-Islamic period, and built a corpus of juridical opinion in regard to the attributes that must be possessed by these two types of financial arrangements to make them fully compatible with the ethos of the value system of Islam. The wealth of Islamic jurisprudence literature on the subject has been of invaluable help in devising models of Islamic banking capable of functioning on truly Islamic lines in the modern age.

In developing models of Islamic banking, scholars of recent times have tried to follow as closely as possible the precepts of the highly respected jurists of the early Islamic period. However, in matters on which the *Qur'an* and the *Sunnah* provide no specific injunctions, they have, where necessary, departed from some of the opinions of jurists of the early Islamic period in order to find practical solutions to modern day problems. This is fully in consonance with the objectives of the *Shari'ah* and aids the growth of Islamic jurisprudence to meet the challenges of the modern age. The efforts of Muslim scholars in developing models of banking within the parameters of Islamic teachings had led to a variety of proposals. It will suffice, for purposes of this research, to note the salient features of these models.

The hardcore of almost all the Islamic banking models developed so far is a two-tier mudarabah contract, the first between the depositors and the bank, and the second between the bank and the parties to whom finance is provided. The earliest contributions on the subject were of the nature of summary proposals and had very few details. With the passage of time, increased attention has been given to the details of the operating procedures of Islamic banking, imparting greater degree of realism to the theoretical models.

The earlier Islamic banking models envisaged three main sources of funds for Islamic banks and four principal usage of these funds. The three sources of funds were identified as: (i) the bank's share capital, (ii) mudarabah deposits, and (iii) demand deposits. The four principal uses of these funds were identified as: (i) mudarabah financing, (ii) financing on the basis of the principles of musharakah, (iii) purchase of ordinary shares of commercial or industrial enterprises as well as any investment certificates issued in the private or public sector on profit/loss sharing basis, and (iv) qard al-hasanah. Later models took cognizance of the fact that Islamic banks may need to branch into certain other activities to deploy their funds.

The theoreticians noted that in the actual practice of Islamic banking, a number of Islamic banks that had started operating in the 1970s in different countries did not confine their activities to only the four modes of finance envisaged in the earlier theoretical models. The *Shari'ah* experts associated with the working of these banks saw no objection to banks engaging in activities like murabahah (a contract in which a client wishing to purchase equipment or goods requests the bank to purchase the items and sell them to him at cost plus a declared profit), bai muajjal (a trade deal in which the seller allows the buyer to pay the price of a commodity at a future date in lump sum or in instalments), ijara (leasing), ijara wa iqtina (hire purchase) and bai salam (advance cash purchases of products). Similarly, banks could also engage in actual conduct of business either on their own or through their wholly-owned subsidiaries. The later models of Islamic banking make specific mention of such activities. This represents a concrete example of the interaction between the theory and practice of Islamic banking.

While delineating the operating procedures of Islamic banks, the theoretical models of Islamic banking have given special attention to the principles governing the allocation of profits between the banks and the mudarabah deposit holders and between the banks and the users of bank funds under profit/loss sharing arrangements. In most of the earliest models, shareholders equity and mudarabah deposits were deemed to be the only two remunerable liabilities of an Islamic bank, and holders of mudarabah deposits were treated as one homogeneous group. The profit sharing arrangements between these two broad groups of providers of capital were envisaged along the following lines:

- The aggregate profit earned by the bank on the total capital will be divided over it. After such a division, the bank will keep an agreed proportion of the profit and the rest will be given to the holders of mudarabah deposits. The proportion of profit division will be determined with the mutual consent of the two parties concerned.
- If the bank suffers a loss, the loss will be shared between the two parties in strict proportion to the capital supplied by each party.
- The maximum incidence of loss to mudarabah deposit holder in a loss situation will be limited to the amount of

his deposit.

In later contributions to the literature on Islamic banking, it was recognized that profit sharing arrangements among the remunerable liabilities of an Islamic bank could take more complex forms while still remaining within the *Shari'ah* parameters. It was felt that there was a strong case for some flexibility in profit sharing ratios depending upon the degree of risk to which various types of remunerable liabilities were exposed. [1] The mudarabah deposits of a longer maturity could be given an edge over deposits of shorter maturity in the profit sharing arrangements. Similarly, a distinction could be made between the providers of redeemable capital and non-redeemable capital, with provision of larger return to providers of non-redeemable capital.

As for the profit sharing arrangements between the bank and the users of bank funds, Islamic banking models stick to the basic principle laid down in the *Shari'ah* that profit earned from mudarabah business will be distributed between the provider of funds (the bank) and the user of bank funds on the basis of proportions settled in advance. No fixed amount can be settled for any party, and loss, if any, unless caused by negligence or violation of the terms of the contract by the user of bank funds, will be borne by the provider of funds. For the purpose of profit/loss sharing in musharakah business, the respective capital contributions of parties, utilized for varying periods, would be brought to a common denomination by multiplying the amounts with the number of days during which each particular item such as equity capital of a firm, its current cash surpluses, suppliers credit as well as the finance provided by the bank were actually deployed in the business. In other words, the calculation of the respective capital contributions of the parties would be made on a daily product basis.

A prominent feature of Islamic banking models is the relegation of loans and advances to a very minor role whereas they play a dominant role in the assets structure of the interest based banks. This is for the simple reason that no return is allowed on loans and advances in the Islamic system whereas in the conventional system, they are high return assets. The use of lending is confined mainly to help meet the needs of those who are unable to secure financing facility in any other way.

While profit/loss sharing is the central feature of almost all the Islamic banking models developed so far, various writers have expressed differing viewpoints on certain aspects of the working of Islamic banks. It has been suggested that Islamic banks should draw a sharp distinction between money deposited as demand deposits and money deposited in mudarabah accounts. Demand deposits should be backed by 100 percent reserve as they are of the nature of an amanah (safe keeping). [2] This view is not shared by others who regard demand deposits as qard al-hasanah deposits whose repayment in full on demand is guaranteed by the bank but these can be used by the bank in its financing operations.

Some important viewpoints are indicated below.

1. Some writers are of the view that Islamic banks should not resort to credit creation. [3] They feel that credit creation enables banks to reap unjustified profits, which go to enrich a limited class of population. Others see no objection to credit creation by the Islamic banks and are of the view that means can be found to ensure that the benefits from the totality of banking operations are equitably distributed.

2. Some writers are of the view that for Islamic banks to really work in the Islamic spirit it is necessary that they should be small-localized institutions. [4] They feel that Islamic banks should be a decentralized chain of institutions sharing the features of local banks, cooperative society and a social service organization. Others do not go to this extreme but seem to be against big-sized banks to prevent them from exercising undue power. [5] Most other writers are of the view that Islamic banking can be practiced according to its underlying spirit irrespective of the size of the banks.

3. Some writers have suggested that Islamic banks should be required to earmark a certain part of their demand deposits for providing interest free loans to the government to enable it to finance socially beneficial projects for which the required financing cannot be secured on profit sharing basis. [6] The rationale for this is that since the funds available to a bank through demand deposits belong to the public and the banks do not pay any return on these deposits, a part of these should be utilized for meeting the financial needs of the government. Similarly, it has been suggested that a part of demand deposits may be utilized for making interest free loans for meeting genuine consumption requirements of the people. [7] Others are of the view that provision of interest free loans to the government should be undertaken by the central bank of the country rather than the commercial banks. A number of writers have expressed the view that commercial banks should not be involved in financing the consumption requirements of the people. They think that Zakat funds should be used for meeting the consumption requirements of the really needy persons while others should be motivated to set up cooperative self-help bodies to finance the consumption requirements of individual members as the need arises.

The literature on Islamic banking does not deal only with the mechanics of Islamic banking. It delves deep in the philosophy of Islamic banking. It has been pointed out that the monetary and banking system of a country does not operate in an ideological vacuum. It is an integral part of its parent ideology. Its operating procedures have to be fashioned in accordance with the requirements of a particular ideology. Judged in this perspective, the task of the replacement of conventional banking by Islamic banking does not consist of a mere mechanical replacement of interest by non-interest modes of financing.

These modes have to be chosen keeping in view the

religious prescriptions as well as the ideological orientation of an Islamic society. Further, the financing activities of Islamic banks have to be directed towards achieving the Islamic socio-economic objectives. These objectives briefly are promotion of a pattern of growth best suited for eradication of poverty, equitable distribution of income and wealth and sufficient opportunities for gainful employment.

An important policy issue that has been discussed extensively in the above context is whether keeping in view the Islamic teachings and Islamic socio-economic objectives, the Islamic banks should have a preference pattern with respect to various modes of financing which are permissible in Shari'ah. It has been forcefully argued by a number of writers that the real substitute of interest in an Islamic financial system is the mode of profit/loss sharing along with qard al-hasanah while the other techniques like murabahah, bai muajjal, ijara and ijara wa iqtina cannot be of equal significance in achieving the Islamic socio-economic objectives.

The reasoning employed is as follows. Islam disallows the interest system because intrinsically it is a highly inequitable system. The feature that makes the interest system inequitable is that the provider of capital funds is assured a fixed return while all the risk is borne by the user of these capital funds. Justice, which is the hallmark of the Islamic system, demands that the provider of capital funds should share the risk with the entrepreneur if he wishes to earn profit. It follows, therefore, that financing techniques like murabahah, bai muajjal, ijara and ijara wa iqtina, which involve a pre-determined return on capital, cannot be regarded as commendable substitutes for interest, and should only be used sparingly when absolutely needed.

The writings have also emphasized that Islamic banking is expected not only to avoid transaction based on interest, but also to participate actively in achieving Islamic socio-economic objectives of eradication of poverty, achievement of an equitable pattern of income distribution and generation of maximum employment opportunities. It has been argued that these objectives can best be achieved through the profit/loss sharing techniques of mudarabah and musharakah.

The literature on Islamic banking also encompasses central banking and monetary policy. It has been emphasized that, in the initial stages of the integration of Islamic banks in a country's financial system, the main task of central banking would be the promotion of an institutional framework necessary for the smooth operation of financial markets in compliance with the rules of the *Shari'ah*. [9] The central bank would have to play a leading role in the development of new financial instruments for the money and capital markets of an Islamic economy. The new financial instruments that have been suggested in this context include Participation Term Certificates (which would entitle its holders to share in the profits of the concern issuing them), Specific Investment Certificates (which would carry the name of the enterprise in which the proceeds of the certificates would be invested and in whose profit their holders would share) and Leasing Certificates (which would entitle their holders to a proportionate share in the yield of the assets leased by a company net of administrative expenses). [10] It has also been suggested that the central bank may itself issue a distinctive type of investment certificate and invest its proceeds through the banking system. [11] All these certificates may be issued in different denominations and with different maturities to suit the preferences of various groups of savers. It is envisaged that a secondary market will then develop in which the aforesaid types of primary securities will be sold and resold before maturity, imparting liquidity to such securities and widening the choice of investment media available to savers.

While discussing the other responsibilities of the central bank in an Islamic economy, Muslim writers have stressed the need for pursuing monetary policies designed to help achieve Islamic socio-economic objectives. They have emphasized that monetary policy in an Islamic economy cannot afford to be value neutral. The central bank is expected to make a skilful use of monetary policy instruments available to it to influence the operations of the banking system that the egalitarian objectives of an Islamic society are achieved with greater ease.

A conscientious effort has to be made to ensure that the financing provided by the banks makes a positive contribution to eradication of poverty, generation of maximum employment opportunities and achievement of an equitable pattern of income distribution. Another major responsibility of the central bank is to safeguard monetary stability as both inflation and deflation impose a welfare cost on the society and cause severest hardship to the poorest sections of the population.

Considerable attention has been given in the literature to the modifications that would be needed in the actual conduct of monetary policy when a transition is made from an interest-based economy to an interest free economy. In an interest free economy, the central bank will have no use for the traditional monetary policy instrument of changes in the bank rate. Open market operations in the traditional sense of the term will also lose their relevance in an interest free framework. Most other monetary policy instruments available to the conventional central banks will, however, remain usable by a central bank operating on non-interest basis.

Thus, it will be possible for it to set cash reserve requirements for the commercial banks and to vary them as an instrument of monetary policy. It could also impose a liquidity ratio and vary it from time to time in accordance with the needs of the situation. The central bank would also be able to regulate the monetary situation by placing quantitative ceilings on the financing operations of banks. For influencing the flow of bank funds in the desired manner and for encouraging or discouraging the use of bank finance for specified purposes, the central bank will be able to use measures of selective control like restricting the use of bank resources for certain purposes and setting mandatory targets for financial assistance to be provided by banks for stated purposes.

To compensate for the loss of the bank rate weapon, some study groups and scholars have suggested that central banks operating on a non-interest basis may be empowered to vary the profit sharing ratios applicable to various types of financial assistance to be made available by the central bank to the commercial banks. In addition, the central bank may be empowered to prescribe maximum and minimum profit sharing ratios for banks in respect of finance provided by them, which may be varied from time to time if the situation so warrants. [12] Others have not favoured these proposals as they feel that any change in profit sharing ratio after it has been written into a contract, is not permissible under Islamic legal code. [13] However, they would probably not object to change in profit sharing ratios, which apply to future contracts and prescription of a range of differential profit sharing ratios to influence both the overall monetary situation and the pattern of resource allocation.

Regarding open market operations, different opinions have been expressed. Some scholars have ruled out the use of this instrument of monetary policy on account of the absence of a government securities market in an interest free economy. They do not favour open market operations in shares of private concerns for several reasons. [14] It is not desirable, they point out, for the central bank to buy and sell the stocks of private sector companies. Besides, variations in the prices of equity-based instruments brought about by central bank open market operations would benefit or penalize the shareholders of companies whose shares are used for this purpose. This will not be equitable and can introduce distortions in the share market. [15] Others, however, do not rule out the possibility of open market operations and propose issuance of variable divided securities by the central bank related to their profit in which such operations could be conducted.

2.3 Viability of Islamic Banking

A good deal of literature on non-conventional banking is

concerned with the viability of banking institutions, which seek to operate on an interest free basis. Notice has been taken of a number of misgivings expressed about the viability of interest free banking and an effort made to dispel these misgivings. [16] The more important of such misgivings can be stated as follows:

1. Because of commitment to share in losses also, non-conventional banks working on the principle of profit/loss sharing will be exposed to huge losses leading to their failure and insolvency.
2. Non-conventional banks will experience frequent defaults and loss in their earnings on account of concealment of correct income by their clients which will undermine their stability.
3. Islamic banks cannot perform all the banking functions on non-interest basis in a world that is dominated by interest based transactions.

Muslim writers have pointed out that the commitment of Islamic banks to share in losses will not necessarily involve them in huge losses leading to their failure and insolvency. [17] Islamic banks are expected to operate on the basis of a diversified investment portfolio so that notwithstanding losses suffered in some individual cases, the overall profitability can be maintained on account of the pooling of risks. Losses to banks arise mainly on account of defaults on the part of concerns to which finance is provided. There is no intrinsic reason why an Islamic bank should experience more defaults in the fulfilment of contractual obligations on the part of its clientele compared to other banks. [18]

There are three main elements which are germane to the possibility of defaults viz., the nature of the party to whom finance is provided, the purpose for which finance is provided and the type of supervision exercised by the banks on the end-use of funds. These elements are essentially the same for a non-conventional bank and a conventional bank, and if sufficient care is not exercised in regard to these elements, defaults would arise irrespective of whether the bank concerned follows the traditional banking practices or the principles of Islamic banking. Given prudent management, there is no reason to believe that the incidence of defaults would be greater in the case of Islamic banks compared to other banks. [19] On the contrary, one should expect that the incidence of defaults would be less because, on account of their having a direct stake in the profit of concerns to whom finance is provided, Islamic banks would be more vigilant in monitoring the end-use of funds as compared to the traditional banks which attach greater importance to the security pledged against the loans compared to the actual monitoring of the business dealings of their clientele.

The possibility of the stability of Islamic banking being undermined by a tendency on the part of users of bank funds to conceal their true profits has been the subject matter of extended discussion in recent literature. A study on the relative merits and demerits of interest based and PLS (profit/loss sharing) based banking attributes the dominance of interest based banking in the world at large to the problem of existence of the "moral hazard" in PLS based banking even though PLS based banking is superior to interest based banking in several other respects. [20]

In other writings, it is stressed that though the existence of the problem of moral hazard in PLS based banking cannot be denied, its risk potential should not be exaggerated. Even the study just now referred, acknowledges that over time the incentive to cheat would be reduced as loss of reputation would restrict future access to credit markets. Others have pointed out that: (a) under reporting of profits, which is considered as cheating can be challenged in court in the case of *mudarabah* contract, (b) users of bank funds who try to cheat could be blacklisted and denied funds from the banking system as a whole; this would serve as a strong deterrent to under reporting of profit, (c) firm specific and project specific contracts can be developed that elicit optimal behaviour even in the presence of moral hazard, and (d) in cases where the non-disclosure of correct income is due to the complexity of the tax system, corruption in the tax collecting machinery and weaknesses of the audit system, appropriate changes in the tax and audit systems would help in overcoming the problem. [21]

Another misgiving about the feasibility of Islamic banking of which note has been taken by Muslim scholars in that Islamic bank cannot perform all the banking functions on non-interest basis in a world dominated by interest. These scholars recognize that successful conduct of Islamic banking in an international environment that is permeated with interest is of course a big challenge. [22] In the financing of multilateral trade transactions, Islamic banks have of the necessity to deal with conventional banks. In a number of contributions it has been suggested that ways can be found for dealing of Islamic banks with conventional banks on non-interest basis.

It has been suggested, for example, that in establishing correspondent relationship with conventional banks, the following procedure could be adopted: (a) the Islamic banks will keep a reasonable amount of cash in their current account with the correspondent banks, (b) the Islamic banks will endeavour to correct a debit balance in their account with correspondent banks as soon as possible, (c) the correspondent bank will not charge any interest on the temporary debit balances of Islamic banks in lieu of its freedom to use the credit balances of Islamic banks profitably without paying any compensation to the Islamic banks, and (d) as partial security, the correspondent bank, while adding its confirmation to import letters of credit, will debit the Islamic banks only with a certain "cash margin" so that Islamic banks need to keep only such credit balances with correspondent banks as are likely to cover the cash margins of the letters of credit and not the whole value of these letters. [23]

2.4 Socio-economic Consequences of Islamic Banking

The possible socio-economic consequences of Islamic

banking have been the subject matter of extended discussion in recent literature. The discussion has proceeded mainly on the basis of the presumption that profit and loss sharing based modes of financing will have a dominant role in the conduct of Islamic banking while the other modes would be used sparingly. [24] The main focus of discussion has been on the possible impact of Islamic banking on savings, investment, rate and pattern of growth, allocative efficiency and the overall stability of the banking and the economic system.

2.4.1 Effects on Saving and Investment: Concerns have been expressed that adoption of an interest free system may have an adverse effect on saving because of increased uncertainty regarding the rate of return. Muslim economists have pointed out that standard economic analysis does not yield a definitive conclusion regarding the effect of increased uncertainty of rate of return on the quantum of saving. It has been agreed that the actual outcome would depend on a number of factors such as the form of the utility function and its risk properties, for example, the degree and the extent of risk aversion, the degree to which future is discounted, whether or not increased risk is compensated by higher return, and finally the income and substitution effects of increased uncertainty. [25]

It has further been argued that the move to an Islamic interest free system, under certain conditions, could lead to increased rates of return on savings. Consequently, the increased level of uncertainty that could result from adoption of PLS based system could be compensated for by an increased rate of return on savings, leaving the overall level of savings unchanged or perhaps even leading to an increase in savings.

Muslim economists expect PLS based banking to exercise a favourable effect on the level of investment. It has been pointed out that both the demand for investment funds and the supply of investment funds are likely to show an increase consequent to replacement of interest based banking by PLS based banking. [26] The demand for investment funds is likely to increase as a fixed cost of capital is no longer required to be met as a part of the firm's profit calculations. The marginal product of capital can, therefore, be taken up to the point where maximum profits are obtained without the constraint of, meeting a fixed cost of capital. The supply of investment funds is likely to increase as PLS based banking is enabled to undertake the financing of a larger number of risky projects on account of an enhanced risk absorbing capacity.

2.4.2 Impact on the Rate and Pattern of Growth: Several scholars have discussed the likely impact of the adoption of Islamic banking practices on the rate and pattern of growth. It has been pointed out that the expected favourable effect of PLS based banking on the level of investment would impart a pronounced growth orientation to the economy. [27] The increased availability of risk capital under the Islamic system would promote technological innovation and experimentation, which would be another plus factor for growth. Islamic banks are also expected to influence the pattern of growth through appropriate selectivity in their financial operations to ensure that the process of growth is broad based and an optimal use is made of bank resources for purposes which rank high in Islamic socio-economic objectives. It is recognized that the central bank of the country will have to play a strong guiding role in this context. [28]

2.4.3 Impact on Allocative Efficiency: Allocative efficiency of an interest free economy has been an area of major concern in the writings of many Muslim economists. It has been stated that a financial system based on an Islamic framework of profit sharing would be more efficient in allocating resources as compared to the conventional interest based system. This position is defended on the basis of the general proposition that any financial development that causes investment alternatives to be compared to one another, strictly based on their productivity and rates of return, is bound to produce allocative improvements, and such a proposition is the cornerstone of the Islamic financial system.

Muslim economists do not deny that investment efficiency requires the use of discounting to take proper care of the time dimension of costs and benefits. [29] They, however, emphasize that non-existence of interest does not mean that discounting as a technique of computing the present value of future cash flows cannot be used in an interest free economy. It has further been pointed out that interest rate is not the proper discount factor under conditions of uncertainty even in interest based economies. Under conditions of uncertainty, the rate of return on equity is the proper discount rate. Since the real world is a world of uncertainty and since no real investment in any economy can be undertaken without facing risks, cash flows of such investment should be discounted not by a risk less interest rate but by the true opportunity cost of venture capital.

2.4.4 Consequences for the Stability of the Banking System: It has been argued in the literature on Islamic banking "that a switch over from interest based banking to PLS base banking would impart greater stability to the banking system. The argument proceeds on the following lines. In the interest-based system, the nominal value of deposit liabilities is fixed. [30] However, there is no assurance on the assets side that all the loans and advances will be recovered. Shocks on the assets side, therefore, lead to divergence between assets and liabilities, and the banking system can suffer a loss of confidence in the process, leading to banking crises. In the PLS based system, the nominal value of investment deposits is not guaranteed, and shocks to the assets positions are promptly absorbed in the values of investment deposits. This minimizes the risk of bank failures and enhances the stability of the banking system".

2.4.5 Effects on the Stability of the Economic System: The literature on Islamic banking has taken note of apprehensions expressed in certain circles that replacement of interest by profit/loss sharing may make the whole economic system highly unstable as disturbances originating in one part of the economy will be transmitted to the rest of the economy. [31] The general consensus holds such apprehensions to be lacking in substance and suggests, on the contrary, that-elimination of interest, coupled with other institutional features of an Islamic economy, will tend to enhance stability. It has been pointed out that interest based debt financing is a major factor in causing economic instability in capitalist economies. It is easy to see, for example, how the interest based system intensifies business recession.

As soon as the banks find that business concerns are beginning to incur losses, they reduce assistance and call back loans, as a result of which some firms have to close down. This increases unemployment resulting in further reduction in demand, and the infection spreads. Islamic banks, on the other hand, are prepared to share losses, which reduces the severity of business recession and enables the productive enterprises to tide over difficult periods without a shut down. Islamic banking has, therefore, to be regarded as a promoter of stability rather than a conduit of instability. [32]

2.5 The Practice of Islamic Banking

The Islamic banking movement began on a modest scale in the early 1960s. [33] The earliest experiments in Islamic banking took place in most cases on individual initiative with governments playing a more or less passive role. The later growth of the Islamic banking movement has been significant, helped by the encouragement provided by the governments of a number of Muslim countries. The establishment of Islamic banks in a number of countries has been facilitated by special enactments and suitable changes in banking legislation. It should be mentioned that changes in banking legislation affected in certain countries to facilitate the working of Islamic banks vis-à-vis the conventional banks. They are in fact designed to remove some of the handicaps from which Islamic banks suffer in conducting their operations in an economy where interest based transactions dominate the scene.

Two different approaches are discernible in regard to adoption of Islamic banking practices. In a number of countries, Islamic banks have been started on a private initiative. The governments of these countries have not committed themselves to the abolition of interest, and Islamic banks exist side by side with interest-based banks. Pakistan and Iran are following a different approach aimed at economy wide elimination of interest. In Sudan, where Islamic banks co-existed with interest based banks for a long time, the government has now opted for economy wide Islamisation of banking. This section reviews the trends in the practice of Islamic banking in both the settings. It also takes note of the activities of the Islamic Development Bank, which is an international development financing institution working on *Shari'ah* principles, the Islamic banking experiments in some non-Muslim countries, and offer of Islamic banking services by conventional banks in certain Muslim countries.

2.5.1 Practice of Islamic Banking-Individual Entities: There are now over two hundred and fifty Islamic banking institutions operating in different countries encompassing most of the Muslim world. Two major international holding companies, namely, the Dar al-Mal al Islami Trust and the Al-Baraka Group control a number of Islamic banks. Associations of individual sponsors have established most others. In some banks there is also a certain amount of government participation in the share capital. Islamic banks conduct their banking operations under *Shari'ah* principles. Almost all of them have Shari'ah Supervisory Boards as part of their organizational structure. The function of Shari'ah Supervisory Board is to ensure the compatibility of all the operations of Islamic banks with the requirements of *Shari'ah*.

Islamic banks accept both demand deposits and saving and time deposits. Demand deposits are treated as qard al-hasanah. The bank is given permission to use the deposit amounts at its discretion but with guarantee of returning the full principal amount on demand. Saving deposits are differentiated from demand deposits as they are subject to certain restrictions with respect to the amounts that can be withdrawn from such accounts at any one time and the periodicity of such withdrawals. Some Islamic banks accept saving deposits on profit/loss sharing basis while others do not pay any return on these deposits and guarantee the principal amount.

Time deposits are accepted by Islamic banks on profit/loss sharing basis and are generally known as "Investment Accounts" or "Investment Deposits". The investment deposits of Islamic banks can have different maturity periods. The return on investment deposits is specified as a percentage of total profit in most cases, but in some cases, the percentage return varies with the length of the period for which the deposits are made.

Apart from limited period deposits, some Islamic banks also accept unlimited period investment deposits. In this case, the period of deposit is not specified and the deposits are automatically renewed unless a notice of termination of deposits is given of a mutually agreed time interval. Some Islamic banks also have specific investment accounts in which deposits are made for investment in particular projects. The return to depositors in these accounts depends on the outcome of these particular projects and the ratio of profit sharing agreed between the bank and the depositors.

Islamic banks operating in different countries are using a combination of the different financing techniques permissible in *Shari'ah*. However, most of them lean heavily on bai muajjal/murabahah in their operations. This is for two main reasons. Firstly, their orientation mainly is towards short-term financing of trade transactions for which bai muajjal/ murabahah appear to be more convenient devices compared to the system of profit/loss sharing. Secondly, they are in competition with interest-based banks and are therefore anxious to earn at least as much on their investments as will enable them to give a return roughly comparable to prevailing interest rates to their investment account holders. This is easier to achieve by engaging in bai muajjal/murabahah transaction as the "mark-up" can be fixed in a manner which more or less assures the required return. [34] On the other hand, considerable uncertainty attached to earnings under a system of profit/loss sharing, as the outcome depends on the operating results of various business units that are subject to the usual business hazards.

Excepting the three countries where Islamisation of the banking system has taken place on an economy-wide basis, Islamic banks in other countries are at a considerable disadvantage in facing the competition with conventional banks as they cannot avail of the facilities of the money market which operates on the basis of interest. This forces them to work with much higher liquidity ratios, which has implications for their profitability. Islamic banks also face a number of problems in investing their funds internationally as they cannot take advantage of the facilities of the Eurocurrency market and the Eurobond market, which offer ready investment outlets for conventional banks.

Notwithstanding the handicaps from which they suffer, Islamic banks have succeeded in mobilizing large amount of funds. A detailed study of the working of Islamic banks in different countries conducted in the Islamic Research and Training Institute of the Islamic Development Bank sometime back (called IRTI study hereinafter) showed that deposits in almost all Islamic banks were growing at a rapid pace. Two other studies testify the highly successful deposit mobilization by Islamic banks. According to one study [35], the data relating to the period 1980-1986, showed that the relative growth of Islamic banks was better in most cases than the growth of other banks.

This better relative growth resulted in increasing the shares of Islamic banks in total deposits. The same study mentions that quite a few Islamic banks had grown to become financial institutions of a respectable size within a relatively short period of time. Kuwait Finance House, Faisal Islamic Bank of Egypt and Massaraf Faysal Al-Islami of Bahrain had made such rapid progress that they were counted among the seven largest banks of their respective counties within a short period after their establishment. The other study [36] observes as follows, "These early institutions have now matured, and have achieved a considerable degree of success in terms of market penetration. This is all the more remarkable given that the markets in which they were established already had well developed commercial banks; indeed, some markets, especially in the Gulf, were viewed as over-banked."

Islamic banks have generally a good track record of profitability. [37] Like conventional banks, Islamic banks also have had problems in the recovery of their dues during periods of business recession or losses suffered in some investments, which did not pay off but these have not grown to any crisis proportion. The Dar al-Mal al-Islami, which is a holding company for a large number of Islamic banks, did suffer operating losses in 1983 and 1984, and the Kuwait Finance House had a bad year in 1984 when neither the shareholders nor the depositors received a return on their capital. However, both these institutions recovered from the setback in 1985 and showed good profits. There are of course substantial differences in the performance and profitability of individual institutions within the Islamic banking community but this is not surprising because operating conditions and business environment differ widely from country to country and from time to time in the same country.

Islamic banks are expected to contribute positively towards the achievement of a pattern of growth best suited for the eradication of poverty, equitable distribution of income and wealth and sufficient opportunities for gainful employment. Enough information is not available in regard to operations of Islamic banks in different countries to assess whether they have significantly helped in achieving the Islamic egalitarian objectives. The annual reports of some of the Islamic banks do mention that social considerations are given due importance in planning their operations. The charters of many Islamic banks make specific mention of Islamic socio-economic objectives being the guiding force of their activities.

How far these intentions have actually been translated into practice is difficult to judge in the absence of relevant data. However, there are some indicators which lead to the inference that most of the Islamic banks have not been able to give sufficient attention to financing activities of a developmental nature. From the date given in the IRTI study it appeared that most of the finance being provided by the Islamic banks went to the trade sector. In the case of some banks, trade financing constituted up to 90 percent to total financing.

Data relating to the term structure of finance in the same study showed that most Islamic banks concentrated on providing short-term finance of six months or less or medium term finance of one year or less. These data also corroborate that developmental bias is not prominent in their financing operations. However, time series data, which are available for some Islamic banks, show that as a bank grows in age and experience, it tends to bring about a shift in the pattern of its financing operations in favour of both longer duration financing and greater attention to the developmental requirements of agriculture and industry. [38] Similarly, it expands its client base and pays greater attention to its social responsibilities by extending larger assistance to small-scale industries and new employment generating activities. [39]

A. Pakistan: The process of economy-wide Islamisation of the banking system in Pakistan was initiated soon after a declaration by the then President of Pakistan in February 1979 that Government planned to remove interest from the economy within a period of three years and that a decision had been taken to make a beginning in this direction with the elimination of interest from the operations of the House Building Finance Corporation, National Investment Trust and mutual funds of the Investment Corporation of Pakistan.

Within a few months of this announcement, these specialized financial institutions took the necessary steps to reorient their activities on a non-interest basis.

The conversion of the operations of commercial banks to non-interest basis was a much more complex task and took a longer time span. To begin with, steps were taken in January 1981 to set up separate counters for accepting deposits on profit/loss sharing basis in all the domestic branches of the five nationalized commercial banks. The parallel system, in which savers had the option to keep their money with the banks either in interest bearing deposits or PLS deposits, continued to operate till the end of June 1985; as from 1st July 1985, no banking company was allowed to accept any interest bearing deposits except foreign currency deposits which continue to earn interest. As from that date, all deposits accepted by a banking company share in the profit and loss of the banking company; [40] except deposits in current account on which no interest or profit is given and whose capital sum is guaranteed.

The Central Bank of the country had issued instructions specifying twelve modes of financing in which funds mobilized by the banks can be employed. These were broadly classified into three groups: (a) loan financing, (b) trade related modes of financing, and (c) investment modes of financing. Loan financing takes the form either of qard al-hasanah loans give on compassionate grounds free of any interest or service charge (repayable if and when the borrower is able to repay) or of loans with a service charge not exceeding the proportionate cost of the operation. [41]

Trade related modes of financing include the following: (i) purchase of goods by banks and their sale to clients at appropriate mark up in price on deferred payment basis, (ii) purchase of trade bills, (iii) purchase of movable or immovable property by the banks from their clients with buy-back agreement or otherwise, (iv) leasing, (v) hire-purchase, and (vi) financing for development of property on the basis of a development charge. Investment modes of financing include the following: (i) musharaka, (ii) equity participation and purchase of shares, (iii) purchase of participation term certificates [42] and mudarabah certificates, and (iv) rent sharing.

The Central Bank of the country was authorized to fix the minimum annual rate of profit, which banks should keep in view while considering proposals for provision of finance, and the maximum amount rate of profit they may earn. These rates may be changed from time to time. It has also been laid down that should losses occur, those must be shared by all the financiers in proportion to the respective finances provided by them.

A beginning in the direction of introducing the mudarabah technique of financing was made in June 1980 when a law was promulgated under which companies, banks and other financial institutions can register themselves as mudarabah companies and mobilize funds through the issuance of mudarabah certificates. Funds obtained through a mudarabah can only be used in such businesses, which are permitted under the *Shari'ah*, and need prior clearance from a religious board established by the government specifically for the purpose.

To safeguard the banks against under delays and defaults in repayment by parties obtaining finance from them, a new law called the Banking Tribunals Ordinance was promulgated in 1984. The tribunals set up under the Ordinance were required to dispose of all cases within ninety days of the filing of the complaint. Appeals against the verdicts of tribunals can be filed in the High Courts within thirty days but the decrial amount has to be deposited with the High Court of Appeals. In cases where the decree remains unsatisfied beyond a period of thirty days, the tribunals can also impose fines.

Though a number of steps have been taken since 1979 for the elimination of interest from the financial sector in Pakistan, the process of Islamisation is yet to run its full course. Nothing has been done so far to eliminate interest from government transactions. To begin with, commercial banks were precluded from investing PLS deposits in interest bearing government securities. With the withdrawal of this restriction in August 1985, the movement towards an interest free economy has suffered a serious retardation. Another disappointing feature of the situation is the lack of any notable progress in the transition to profit/loss sharing on the assets side of the banking system. [43] The Islamisation process has been marked by another serious deficiency in that no institutional mechanism exists for a continuous scrutiny of the operating procedures of banks and other financial institution from the *Shari'ah* point of view. Individual scholars who have examined these operating procedures have pointed out several areas where the actual banking practices show deviation from *Shari'ah*.

The Federal Shariat Court in one of its judgments has held that the system of mark-up financing as being practiced by bank is not in conformity with the injunctions of Islam. [44] The mandatory targets that are set every year for bank financing of small business, small-scale industry and small farmers are in line with Islam's egalitarian objectives. In the recent past some additional steps have been taken to reduce the concentration of bank finance among big business groups [45] and to expand the availability of bank finance to low income groups [46] but a really strong drive to use the banking system for achieving Islamic socio-economic objectives is yet to be undertaken.

B. Iran: A new banking law was enacted in Iran in August 1983 to replace interest based banking by interest free banking. The law required the banks to convert their deposits to an interest free basis within one year, and their other operations within three years, from the date of the passage of the law, and specified the types of transactions that must constitute the basis for asset and liability acquisition by banks. The law also specified the responsibilities of the central bank under the new system and mechanics of central bank's control over the banking system.

The law allows the banks to accept two types of deposits, viz., qard al-hasanah deposits and term investment deposits. The qard al-hasanah deposits comprise of current as well as savings accounts which differ in their operational rules. The holders of current and savings accounts are guaranteed the safety of their principal amounts and are not entitled to any contractual return. However, banks are permitted to provide incentives to depositors through: (i) grant of prizes in cash or kind, (ii) reduction in or exemption from service charges or agent's fees payable to banks, and (iii) according priority in the use of banking facilities. Holders of term investment deposits are entitled to receive a variable return, depending on the profitability of the projects in which these funds are invested. The law allows the banks to undertake and/or ensure the repayment of the principal amounts of term investment deposits.

The law provides various modes of operation upon which the financing transaction of banks must be based. Banks are obliged to earmark a portion of their resources for grant of qard al-hasanah to help achieve the socio-economic objectives set out in the constitution of the country. [47] Besides qard al-hasanah, banks are authorized to extend financial assistance for productive ventures on profit/loss sharing basis in accordance with the principles of mudarabah and musharakah. Banks are allowed to provide part of the capital of a new joint stock company and also to purchase shares of existing joint stock companies.

Banks are authorized to provide working capital financing to productive units by purchasing raw materials, spare parts and other items on their request for sale to them on the basis of deferred payment in instalments. Purchase of machinery and equipment for sale to their clients on deferred payment basis is also allowed. Another mode is called salaf which is the same as bai Salam and is used for meeting working capital requirements through advance purchase of output. Banks can engage in lease-purchase transactions. They can also provide finance on the basis of jo'aalah (commission for working as agent), mozara'ah (financing of agricultural production) on profit sharing basis, mosa'qaat (financing of orchard production on profit sharing basis). In addition to these modes of financing, banks are permitted to purchase debt instruments of less than one year maturity if these debts are issued against real assets. [48]

In the new set up, the central bank of the country has been given vast authority to control and supervise the operations of the banks. While it continues to have many of the erstwhile credit control weapons which do not involve riba, it has been endowed with new instruments of control to regulate the interest free operations of the banks. These include power to determine: (a) minimum and maximum expected rate of return from various facilities to the banks, (b) minimum and maximum profits shares for banks in their mudarabah and musharakah activities, and (c) maximum rates of commission the banks can charge for investment accounts for which they serve as trustees.

Studies on the progress made in the implementation of the new system show that banks have, in general, adapted well to the new procedures. Problems have been encountered, however, in moving away from traditional short-term trade financing operations and toward profit sharing medium and long-term financing operations. It was expected that with the passage of time, banks would increase their involvement in mudarabah and musharakah financing but this expectation has not been fulfilled. Comparative data for the period 1984-85 to 1989-90 show that the share of mudarabah in total bank financing has actually gone down from 18.1 percent to 10.7 percent. [49] The combined share of "civil partnership" and "legal partnership" has remained almost unchanged at 18 percent over this period. [50] The share of "instalment sales", on the other hand, has gone up from 33.3 percent to 46.4 percent during the same period. [51]

Studies on the Islamic banking experience of Iran have

pointed out that no attempt has been made so far to Islamise the international banking and financial operations. [52] Government continues to borrow from the banks on the basis of a fixed rate of return. [53] It has also been pointed out that some banking practices in Iran are at variance from the practice of Islamic banking in other countries. [54]

A number of studies refer to conscious efforts made in recent years to re-orientate the activities of banks in Iran to achieve Islamic socio-economic objectives. [55] The banking system has been used as an instrument of restructuring the economy, away from services and consumption towards production. Bank financing to the services sector has been drastically curtailed. Banks have reduced financing for the production of luxury goods and commodities with a large import content, while financial assistance for the production of necessary and intermediate goods has been appreciably increased. Financing facilities for the agricultural sector have been considerably expanded. The banking system has also been used as an instrument of income redistribution through the provision of qard al-hasanah loans to low income groups, financing the building of low cost houses, and provision of financing for small-scale agro-business and industrial co-operatives often without stringent collateral requirements.

C. Sudan: The process of the economy-wide Islamisation of the banking system in Sudan has not been smooth and steady. The first attempt to Islamise the entire banking system was made in 1984 when a presidential decree was issued directing all commercial banks to stop interest based dealings with immediate effect and to negotiate the conversion of their then existing interest bearing deposits and advances into Islamically acceptable forms. Foreign transactions were allowed to be continued on the basis of interest for the time being. It is reported that this sudden change forced the banks to adopt the nearest Islamic alternative available that is, murabahah, which soon constituted 90 percent of their financial operations. [56]

It is also reported that "conventional banks applied Islamic financing techniques only formally in their ledger books and in the reports submitted to the Central Bank of the country. Policy makers in the Central Bank were also discontented with the procedure of transforming the banking system. They considered it as a mere political decision imposed by the government without being preceded by adequate detailed studies. [57] This experiment with economy-wide Islamisation of banking system came to an end in 1985 with the change in government. The government which is presently in power has decided on the economy-wide Islamisation of the banking system once again, and newspaper reports indicate that the effort is much more earnest and much better organized this time.

D. Islamic Development Bank: The Islamic Development Bank, established in 1975, is an international financial institution whose purpose is to foster the economic development and social progress of member countries and Muslim communities individually as well as jointly in accordance with the principles of *Shari'ah*. It has 56 members and a subscribed capital of 6.44 billion Islamic dinars. [58] The functions of the Bank are to participate in the equity capital and grant loans for productive projects in member countries and to provide financial assistance in other forms for economic and social development. The Bank is also required to establish and operate special funds for specific purposes including a fund for assistance to Muslim communities in non-member countries.

The Bank is authorized to accept deposits and to raise funds in any other manner. It is also charged with the responsibility of assisting in the promotion of foreign trade, especially in capital goods, among member countries, providing technical assistance to member countries, extending training facilities for personnel engaged in development activities and undertaking research for enabling the economic, financial and banking activities in Muslim countries to conform to the *Shari'ah*.

Following the continuous growth of the Bank financing operations to support efforts for economic development in member countries, the Bank has sought to mobilize additional resources. An Investment Deposit Scheme was initiated in 1980 under which deposits are accepted from institutions and individuals for use in foreign trade financing operations. An Islamic Banks' portfolio was created in 1987 which aims at mobilizing liquid funds of Islamic banks and financial institutions. The IDB Unit Investment Fund was launched in 1989 to generate additional financial resources for the Bank and to invest them on a basis compatible with the *Shari'ah*.

The cumulative financing approved by the Bank since its inception till the end of 1991-92 amounted to 9389.13 million Islamic dinars. Foreign trade financing, based on murabahah, has accounted for bulk of the total resources provided by the Bank to its members. It accounted for 72.5 percent of total financing. Loans provided on the basis of a service charge accounted for 8.2 percent while leasing and instalment sales accounted for 5.3 percent and 6.3 percent of total financing respectively. Equity participation accounted for a mere 2.2 percent of total financing while the assistance provided through profit sharing was quantitatively even less significant, accounting for a meagre 0.2 percent of total financing.

Equity participation and profit sharing are regarded as the chief distinguishing feature of Islamic banking and finance. It is disappointing to note, therefore, that they have so far played a very minor role in the financing operations of the Islamic Development Bank. A detailed study of the working of the Bank by one of its former principal officer's points out that it "started its equity financing operations enthusiastically and gradually built up this activity to its highest level in the year 1401H. However, since then, operations have dropped sharply in view of the Bank's unhappy experience with several of its equity investments". [59]

The same study also analyses the reasons for this unhappy

experience. The over-anxiety of the Bank in its initial years to expand the network of equity financing to cover as many of its member countries as possible, lack of sufficient professional expertise in the Bank to undertake an adequate appraisal of projects and to pursue the task of vigorous follow-up of its equity investments, delay in the implementation of projects financed by the Bank, marketing difficulties and currency devaluation have been cited as the main factors responsible for this situation. [60] It is reported that the Bank is engaged in devising corrective measures and safeguards and equipping itself better for undertaking equity financing by directing greater attention to the macro economic conditions and policies affecting the projects, stricter supervision and linking disbursements to project implementation. [61]

Islamic banking in non-muslim countries and offer of Islamic banking services by conventional banks in Muslim countries encompasses some interesting experiments of what may well be called institutionalized use of Islamic modes of deposit mobilization and financing, if not full-fledged Islamic banking, in quite a few non-Muslim countries. Thus, Islamic financial institutions exist in countries so far apart as Australia, Denmark, India, Liberia, Liechtenstein, Luxembourg, Philippines, South Africa, Thailand, United Kingdom and the United States of America. Apart from these, there are a number of non-Islamic financial institutions in non-Muslim countries which offer Islamic financial services for their Muslim clients. [62] There is a good deal of controversy, however, about the financial services being offered by such institutions being in full conformity with *Shari'ah* requirements. [63]

2.6 Conclusion

Hence, it could be concluded from the above discussion that the demand for Islamic banking services is so strong and persistent among the Muslim masses that authorities in certain Muslim countries have given permission to conventional banks to open "Islamic banking windows". This has been the case in Egypt for quite some time. Recently, such permission has also been accorded in Saudi Arabia and Malaysia.

End Notes

1. M. Nejatullah Siddiqi, (1983), Muslim Economic Thinking: A Survey of Contemporary Literature.
2. Mohsin S. Khan, "Islamic Interest-Free Banking: A Theoretical Analysis" in Mohsin S. Khan and Abbas Mirakhor (eds.), Theoretical Studies in Islamic Banking and Finance (1987).
3. Monzer Kahf, The Islamic Economy (1987) and Ma'bid Ali Al-Jarhi, "A Monetary and Financial Structure for an Interest-Free Economy" in Ziauddin Ahmad et al. (eds.), Money and Banking in Islam (1983).
4. Ahmed al Najjar is the most forceful exponent of this view. Most of his writings are in Arabic. This is a condensation of his views scattered over many writings.
5. M. Umer Chapra, Towards a Just Monetary System (1985), pp. 157-58.
6. Ibid., pp. 161-62.
7. M. Nejatullah Siddiqi, Banking Without Interest (1983), pp. 159-60.
8. M. Nejatullah Siddiqi, Issues in Islamic Banking (1983), pp. 134-140, and Ziauddin Ahmad, Concept and Models of Islamic Banking: An Assessment, papers presented at a seminar on Islamisation of Banking (1984).
9. Abbas Mirakhor, Some Theoretical Aspects of an Islamic Financial System, paper presented at a conference on Islamic Banking (1986), pp. 36-38.
10. Ma'bid Ali Al-Jahri, A Monetary and Financial Structure for an Interest Free Economy, op. cit.
11. Ibid.
12. Council of Islamic Ideology, Report on the Elimination of Interest from the Economy (1980), p. 73.
13. M. Umer Chpra, Towards a Just Monetary System, op. cit, pp. 202-203.
14. Ibid., pp. 204-205.
15. Ziauddin Ahmad, "Some Misgivings about Islamic interest free banking", paper presented in the Annual Lecture Series of Faisal Islamic Bank of Sudan (1985), M. Umer Chapra, Towards a Just

Monetary System, op. cit., pp. 107-139 and M. Nejatullah Siddiqi, Issues in Islamic Banking, op. cit., pp. 59-61.

16. Waqar Masood Khan, Towards an Interest Free Islamic Economic System (1985).

17. Boualem Bendjilali, Book Review of Waqar Masood Khan, Towards an Interest Free Islamic Economic System, in Review of Islamic Economics, Vol. 1, No. 1, 1991, p. 69.

18. M. Nejatullah Siddiqi, "Islamic Banking: Theory and Practice" in M. Ariff (ed.), Islamic Banking in Southeast Asia (1988), p. 53.

19. Abbas Mirakhor, "Some Theoretical Aspects of an Islamic Financial System", op. cit., p. 17, and Nadeem ul Haque and Abbas Mirakhor, "Optimal Profit-Sharing Contracts and Investment in an Interest Free Economy" in Mohsin S. Khan and Abbas Mirakhor (eds.), Theoretical Studies in Islamic Banking and Finance, op. cit., p. 158.

20. Ziauddin Ahmad, "Some Misgivings about Islamic Interest Free Banking", op. cit. pp. 13-14.

21. Abdur Rahim Hamdi, Islamic Banking: Conceptual Framework and Practical Operations (1992), pp. 13-14.

22. Fredric L. Pryor, "The Islamic Economic System", Journal of Comparative Economics (1985), pp. 197-223.

23. Zubair Iqbal and Abbas Mirakhor, Islamic Banking (1987), p. 5.

24. Nadeem Ul Haque and Abbas Mirakhor, "Optimal Profit-Sharing Contracts and Investment in an Interest Free Islamic Economy", op. cit.

25. For some important contributions on the subject, the study by Nadeem Ul Haque and Abbas Mirakhor mentioned in the preceding note as also M. Umer Chapra, Towards a Just Monetary System, op. cit., pp. 111-117, and M. Nejatullah Siddiqi, Issues in Islamic Banking, op. cit., pp. 88-89.

26. The risk absorbing capacity of banks is enhanced in the PLS based system as the nominal value of investment deposits is not guaranteed and banks are not bound to pay a pre-determined return on such deposits.

27. M. Umer Chapra, Towards a Just Monetary System, op. cit., pp. 122-125, and Abul Hasan M. Sadeq, "Economic Growth in an Islamic Economy" in Abul Hasan M. Sadeq et al. (eds.), Development and Finance in Islam (1991), pp. 55-71.

28. Especially, M. Anas Zarqa, "Capital Allocation, Efficiency and

Growth in an Interest Free Islamic Economy" in Journal of Economics and Administration (1982), pp. 43-55.

29. For an elaboration of this theme, see M. Anas Zarqa, "An Islamic Perspective on the Economics of Discounting in Project Evaluation" in Ziauddin Ahmad et al. (eds.), Fiscal Policy and Resource Allocation in Islam (1983), pp. 203-234.

30. For a lucid exposition of this proposition, see Mohsin S. Khan, "Islamic Interest Free Banking: A Theoretical Analysis" in Mohsin S. Khan and Abbas Mirkhor (ed.), Theoretical Studies in Islamic Banking and Finance, op. cit., pp. 15-35.

31. For an expression of the apprehension, see S.N.H. Naqvi, Ethics and Economics: An Islamic Synthesis (1981), p. 136.

32. M. Anas Zarqa, "Stability in an Interest-Free Islamic Economy: A Note" in the Pakistan Journal of Applied Economics, Winter, (1983), pp. 181-188.

33. The Mit-Ghamr Savings Bank, established in 1963 in provincial rural centre in the Nile delta of Egypt, is considered to be the first Islamic bank in modern times. The bank's operations, which were based on the Shari'ah, covered five areas: deposit accounts, loan accounts, equity participation, direct investment, and social services. Though the experiment was localized, the nine branches opened by the bank attracted a very large number of clients and generated a lot of popular enthusiasm.

34. Ausaf Ahmad, Development and Problems of Islamic Banks (1987).

35. Volker Nienhaus, "The Performance of Islamic Banks: Trends and Cases" in Chibli Mallat, Islamic Law and Finance (1988), pp. 83-122.

36. Rodney Wilson (ed.), Islamic Financial Markets (1990), p. 7.

37. For data on profitability of Islamic Banks, see Ausaf Ahmad, Development and Problems of Islamic Banks, op. cit., pp. 51-62, and Volker Nienhaus, "The Performance of Islamic Banks: Trends and Cases" in Chibli Mallat, Islamic Law and Finance, op. cit., pp. 95-108.

38. Albagkir Y. Mudawi, "Islamic Medium and Long-term Finance", Arabia, August 1986.

39. Osman Ahmed, "Sudan: The Role of the Faisal Islamic Bank" in Rodney Wilson (ed.), Islamic Financial Markets, op. cit., pp. 92-97.

40. The rates of profit are worked out by a formula that determines

net profit accruing to a bank and allocates to remunerable liabilities according to their maturities. Allocations are based on differential weights assigned to liabilities according to relative maturities.

41. The central bank of the country has laid down that the maximum rate of service charge which a bank may recover on such loans during an accounting year is to be calculated by dividing the total of its expenses, excluding cost of funds and provision relating to bad assets and income taxation, by the mean of its total assets at the beginning and the end of the year and rounding off the result to the nearest decimal for a percentage point.

42. Participation Term Certificates are negotiable instruments designed to replace debentures for meeting medium and long term financing requirements of business concerns. Instead of receiving interest, as in the case of debentures, the holders of these certificates share in the profit or loss of concerns raising finance through this device. For more details, see Ziauddin Ahmad, "The Present State of Islamic Finance Movement", paper presented at a conference on Islamic Banking in New York (Islamabad, International Institute of Islamic Economics, 1985).

43. The central bank of the country has not yet started publishing data on a regular basis on the shifts in banks assets structure and use being made of various modes of financing. The last published data on this subject relate to December, 1984. These show that equity participation and musharakah financing accounted for only 10 percent and 4 percent respectively of total financing. For details, see Zubair Iqbal ad Abbas Mirakhor, Islamic banking (1987), op. cit. p. 20.

44. Some appeals have been filed against the decree of the Federal Shariat Court and the case is pending before the Shariat Appellate Bench of the Supreme Court of Pakistan.

45. A set of Prudential Regulations for banks were issued by the central bank of the country in 1992 which aim, among other things, to limit bank financing to any single person and to link a fir's access to bank finance to the firm's equity.

46. A scheme for expanding the availability of bank finance for unemployed persons to enable them to own transport vehicles for hire was initiated in 1992.

47. The law stipulates that rules and regulations relating to grant of

qard al-hasanah will be dran up by the central bank of the country and approved by the Council of Ministers.

48. For more details about the various modes of financing in use in Ira, see Zubair Iqbal and Abbas Mirkhor, Islamic Banking, op. cit., pp. 10-11.

49. See S.A.A. Hedayati, "Some Theoretical and Philosophical Aspects of Islamic Banking: A Dimension of Islamic Economics", paper presented at a course in Islamic banking (1992), p. 43.

50. Ibid.

51. Ibid.

52. S.H. Amin, Islamic Law and its Implications for the Modern World (1989), p. 135.

53. In one of the studies it is stated, "In the case of the Islamic Republic of Ira, it has been decreed that financial transactions between ad among the elements of the public sector, including Bank Markazi and commercial banks that are wholly nationalized, can take place on the basis of a fixed rate of return; such a fixed rate is not viewed as interest. Therefore, the government can borrow from the nationalized baking system without violating the injunction of the Law". See Zubair Iqbal and Abbas Mirakhor, Islamic Banking, op. cit., p. 24.

54. A case in point is the treatment of investment deposits. In Iran, the law allows the nominal value of such deposits to be guaranteed while such a guarantee is not considered compatible with Islamic teaching in other countries.

55. Abbas Mirakhor, "The Progress of Islamic Banking: The Case of Iran and Pakistan" in Chibli Mallat, Islamic Law and Finance, op. cit., p. 55 and Mohsin S. Khan, "The Theory and Practice of Islamic Banking", paper presented at a course in Islamic Banking (1992), p. 21.

56. This is reported I a paper presented in Arabic at a conference in Tunis in 1985 which finds a mention in M. Nejatullah Siddiqi, "Islamic Banking: Theory and Practice", op. cit. p. 49.

57. Osman Ahmed, "Sudan: The Role of the Faisal Islamic Bank" in Rodney Wilson (ed.), Islamic Financial Markets, op. cit. p. 77.

58. One Islamic Dinar is equal to one Special Drawing Right (SDR) of the International Monetary Fund.

59. S.A. Meenai, The Islamic Development Bank: A Case Study of Islamic Cooperation (1989), p. 74.

60. Ibid., pp. 74-77.
61. Ibid., pp. 199-200.
62. Among these are such well-known institutions as Kleinworth Benson which offers an Islamic Unit Trust, and the Union Bank of Switzerland and Lander bank of Vienna which offer Islamic investment funds.
63. Rodney Wilson (ed.), Islamic Financial Markets, op. cit. p. 29.

3

Islamic Banking:
Conceptual and Empirical Framework

3.1 Evolution of Islamic Banking

Islamic banking is a new phenomenon that has taken many observers by surprise. The whole banking system has been islamized in both Iran and Pakistan. In addition, there are some thirty Islamic banks in operation in other parts of the globe; including the Jeddah-based Islamic Development Bank (IDB) but excluding numerous non-bank Islamic financial institutions. [1] What is more, the speed with which Islamic banks have sprung up and the rate at which they have progressed make it worth-while to study them systematically.

The first modern experiment with Islamic banking was undertaken in Egypt under cover, without projecting an Islamic image, for fear of being seen as a manifestation of Islamic fundamentalism which was anathema to the political regime. The pioneering effort, led by Ahmad El Najjar, took the form of a savings bank based on profit-sharing in the Egyptian town of Mit Ghamr in 1963.

This experiment lasted until 1967 [2], by which time there were nine such banks in the country. These banks which neither charged nor paid interest, invested mostly by engaging in trade and industry, directly or in partnership with others, and shared the profits with their depositors. [3] Thus, they functioned essentially as saving-investment institutions rather than as commercial banks. The Nasir Social Bank, established in Egypt in 1971, was declared an interest-free commercial bank, although its charter made no reference to Islam or Shariah (Islamic law). The IDB was established in 1974 by the Organization of Islamic Countries (OIC), but it was primarily an inter-governmental bank aimed at providing funds for development projects in member countries. The IDB provides fee-based financial services and profit-sharing financial assistance to member countries. The IDB operations are free of interest and are explicitly based on *Shari'ah* Principles.

3.1.1 *Shari'ah* **Principles:** In the seventies, changes took place in the political climate of many Muslim countries so that there was no longer any strong need to establish Islamic financial institutions under cover. A number of Islamic banks, both in letter and spirit, came into existence in the Middle East, e.g., the Dubai Islamic Bank (1975), the Faisal Islamic Bank of Sudan (1977), the Faisal Islamic Bank of Egypt (1977), and the Bahrain Islamic Bank (1979), to mention a few. The Asia-Pacific region was not oblivious to the winds of change.

The Philippine Amanah Bank (PAB) was established in 1973 by a Presidential Decree as a specialized banking institution without reference to its Islamic character in the bank's charter. The establishment of the PAB was a response by the Philippines Government to the Muslim rebellion in the south, designed to serve the special banking needs of the Muslim community. However, the primary task of the PAB was to assist rehabilitation and reconstruction in Mindanao, Sulu and Palawan in the south. [4] The PAB has eight branches located in the major cities of the southern Muslim provinces, including one in Makati (Metro Manila), in addition to the head office located at Zamboanga City in Mindanao. The PAB, however, is not strictly an Islamic bank, since interest-based operations continue to co-exist with the Islamic modes of financing. It is indeed fascinating to observe that the PAB operates two 'windows' for deposit transactions, i.e., conventional and Islamic. Nevertheless, efforts are underway to convert the PAB into a full-fledged Islamic bank.

Islamic banking made its debut in Malaysia in 1983, but not without antecedents. The first Islamic financial institution in Malaysia was the Muslim Pilgrims Savings Corporation set up in 1963 to help people save for performing Haj (pilgrimage to Mecca and Medina). In 1969, this body evolved into the

Pilgrims Management and Fund Board or the Tabung Haji as it is now popularly known. The Tabung Haji has been acting as a finance company that invests the savings of would-be pilgrims in accordance with *Shari'ah*, but its role is rather limited, as it is a non-banking financial institution. The success of the Tabung Haji, however, provided the main impetus for establishing Bank Islam Malaysia Berhad (BIMB) which represents a full- fledged Islamic commercial bank in Malaysia. The Tabung Haji also contributed 12.5 percent of BIMB's initial capital of M$80 million. BIMB has a complement of fourteen branches in several parts of the country. Plans are afoot to open six new branches a year so that by 1990 the branch network of BIMB will total thirty-three. [5]

Reference should also be made to some Islamic financial institutions established in countries where Muslims are a minority. There was a proliferation of interest-free savings and loan societies in India during the seventies. The Islamic Banking System (now called Islamic Finance House), established in Luxembourg in 1978, represents the first attempt at Islamic banking in the Western world. There is also an Islamic Bank International of Denmark, in Copenhagen, and the Islamic Investment Company has been set up in Melbourne, Australia.

3.2 Essential Feature of Islamic Banking

The essential feature of Islamic banking is that it is interest-free. Although it is often claimed that there is more to Islamic banking, such as contributions towards a more equitable distribution of income and wealth, and increased equity participation in the economy [6], it nevertheless derives its specific rationale from the fact that there is no place for the institution of interest in the Islamic order. Islam prohibits Muslims from taking or giving interest (riba) regardless of the purpose for which such loans are made and regardless of the rates at which interest is charged. To be sure, there have been attempts to distinguish between usury and interest and between loans for consumption and for production. It has also been argued that riba refers to usury practiced by petty money-lenders and not to interest charged by modern banks' and that no riba is involved when interest is imposed on productive loans, but these arguments have not won acceptance. Apart from a few dissenting opinions, the general consensus among Muslim scholars clearly is that there is no difference between riba and interest. In what follows, these two terms are used interchangeably.

The prohibition of riba is mentioned in four different revelations in the *Qur'an*. [7] The first revelation emphasizes that interest deprives wealth of God's blessings. The second revelation condemns it, placing interest in juxtaposition with wrongful appropriation of property belonging to others. The third revelation enjoins Muslims to stay clear of interest for the sake of their own welfare. The fourth revelation establishes a clear distinction between interest and trade, urging Muslims to take only the principal sum and to forgo even this sum if the borrower is unable to repay. It is further declared in the *Qur'an* that those who disregard the prohibition of interest are at war with God and His Prophet. The prohibition of interest is also cited in no uncertain terms in the Hadith (sayings of the Prophet). The Prophet condemned not only those who take interest but also those who give interest and those who record or witness the transaction, saying that they are all alike in guilt. [8]

It may be mentioned in passing that similar prohibitions are to be found in the pre-*Qur'anic* scriptures, although the 'People of the Book', as the *Qur'an* refers to them, had chosen to rationalize them. It is amazing that Islam has successfully warded off various subsequent rationalization attempts aimed at legitimizing the institution of interest. Some scholars have put forward economic reasons to explain why interest is banned in Islam. It has been argued, for instance, that interest, being a pre-determined cost of production, tends to prevent full employment. [9] In the same vein, it has been contended that international monetary crises are largely due to the institution of interest, and that trade cycles are in no small measure attributable to the phenomenon of interest. None of these studies, however, has really succeeded in establishing a causal link between interest, on the one hand, and employment and trade cycles, on the other.

Others, anxious to vindicate the Islamic position on interest, have argued that interest is not very effective as a monetary policy instrument even in capitalist economies and have questioned the efficacy of the rate of interest as a determinant of saving and investment. [10] A common thread running through all these discussions is the exploitative character of the institution of interest, although some have pointed out that profit (which is lawful in Islam) can also be exploitative. One response to this is that one must distinguish between profit and profiteering, and Islam has prohibited the latter as well.

Some writings have alluded to the 'unearned income' aspect of interest payments as a possible explanation for the Islamic doctrine. The objection that rent on property is considered halal (lawful) is then answered by rejecting the analogy between rent on property and interest on loans, since the benefit to the tenant is certain, while the productivity of the borrowed capital is uncertain. Besides, property rented out is subject to physical wear and tear, while money lent out is not. The question of erosion in the value of money and hence the need for indexation is an interesting one. But the Islamic jurists have ruled out compensation for erosion in the value of money, or, according to Hadith, a fungible good must be returned by its like (mithl): 'gold for gold, silver for silver, wheat for wheat, barley for barley, dates for dates, salt for salt, like for like, equal for equal, and hand to hand...' [11]

The bottom line is that Muslims need no 'proofs' before they reject the institution of interest–no human explanation for a divine injunction is necessary for them to accept a dictum, as they recognize the limits to human reasoning. No human mind can fathom a divine order; therefore it is a matter of faith (iman).

The Islamic ban on interest does not mean that capital is costless in an Islamic system. Islam recognizes capital as a factor of production but it does not allow the factor to make a prior or pre-determined claim on the productive surplus in the form of interest. This obviously poses the question as to what will then replace the interest rate mechanism in an Islamic framework. There have been suggestions that profit-sharing can be a viable alternative. [12] In Islam, the owner of capital can legitimately share the profits made by the entrepreneur. What makes profit-sharing permissible in Islam, while interest is not, is that in the case of the former it is only the profit-sharing ratio, not the rate of return itself that is pre-determined.

It has been argued that profit-sharing can help allocate resources efficiently, as the profit-sharing ratio can be influenced by market forces so that capital will flow into those sectors which offer the highest profit-sharing ratio to the investor, other things being equal. One dissenting view is that the substitution of profit-sharing for interest as a resource allocating mechanism is crude and imperfect and that the institution of interest should therefore be retained as a necessary evil. However, mainstream Islamic thinking on this subject clearly points to the need to replace interest with something else, although there is no clear consensus on what form the alternative to the interest rate mechanism should take. The issue is not resolved and the search for an alternative continues, but it has not detracted from efforts to experiment with Islamic banking without interest.

3.3 Anatomy of Islamic Banking

As mentioned earlier, Islam does not deny that capital, as a factor of production, deserves to be rewarded. Islam allows the owners of capital a share in a surplus which is uncertain. To put it differently, investors in the Islamic order have no right to demand a fixed rate of return. No one is entitled to any addition to the principal sum if he does not share in the risks involved. The owner of capital (rabbul-mal) may 'invest' by allowing an entrepreneur with ideas and expertise to use the capital for productive purposes and he may share the profits, if any, with the entrepreneur-borrower (mudarib); losses, if any, however, will be borne wholly by the rabbul-mal. This mode of financing, termed mudaraba in the Islamic literature was in practice even in the pre-Qur'anic days and, according to jurists, it was approved by the Prophet.

Another legitimate mode of financing recognized in Islam is one based on equity participation (musharaka) in which the partners use their capital jointly to generate a surplus. Profits or losses will be shared between the partners according to some agreed formula depending on the equity ratio. Mudaraba and musharaka constitute, at least in principle if not in practice, the twin pillars of Islamic banking. The musharaka principle is invoked in the equity structure of Islamic banks and is similar to the modern concepts of partnership and joint stock ownership. In so far as the depositors are concerned, an Islamic bank acts as a mudarib which manages the funds of the depositors to generate profits subject to the rules of mudaraba as outlined above.

The bank may in turn use the depositors' funds on a mudaraba basis in addition to other lawful modes of financing. In other words, the bank operates a two-tier mudaraba system in which it acts both as the mudarib on the saving side of the equation and as the rabbul-mal on the investment portfolio side. The bank may also enter into musharaka contracts with the users of the funds, sharing profits and losses, as mentioned above. At the deposit end of the scale, Islamic banks normally operate three broad categories of account, mainly current, savings, and investment accounts. The current account, as in the case of conventional banks, gives no return to the depositors.

It is essentially a safe-keeping (al-wadiah) arrangement between the depositors and the bank, which allows the depositors to withdraw their money at any time and permits the bank to use the depositors' money. As in the case of conventional banks, cheque books are issued to the current account deposit holders and the Islamic banks provide the broad range of payment facilities—clearing mechanisms, bank drafts, bills of exchange, traveller cheques, etc. (but not yet, it seems, credit cards or bank cards). More often than not, no service charges are made by the banks in this regard.

The savings account is also operated on an al-wadiah basis, but the bank may at its absolute discretion pay the depositors a positive return periodically, depending on its own profitability. Such payment is considered lawful in Islam since it is not a condition for lending by the depositors to the bank, nor is it pre-determined. The savings account holders are issued with savings books and are allowed to withdraw their money as and when they please. The investment account is based on the mudaraba principle, and the deposits are term deposits which cannot be withdrawn before maturity. The profit-sharing ratio varies from bank to bank and from time to time depending on supply and demand conditions. [13] In theory, the rate of return could be positive or negative, but in practice the returns have always been positive and quite comparable to rates conventional banks offer on their term deposits. [14]

At the investment portfolio end of the scale, Islamic banks employ a variety of instruments. The mudaraba and musharaka modes, referred to earlier, are supposedly the main conduits for the outflow of funds from the banks. In practice, however, Islamic banks have shown a strong preference for other modes which are less risky. The most commonly used mode of financing seems to be the 'mark-up' device which is termed murabaha.

In a murabaha transaction, the bank finances the purchase of a good or asset by buying it on behalf of its client and adding a mark-up before re-selling it to the client on a 'cost-plus' basis. It may appear at first glance that the mark-up is just another term for interest as charged by conventional banks, interest thus being admitted through the back door. What makes the murabaha transaction Islamically legitimate is that the bank first acquires the asset and in the process it assumes certain risks between purchase and resale. The bank takes responsibility for the good before it is safely delivered to the client. The services rendered by the Islamic bank are therefore regarded as quite different from those of a conventional bank which simply lends money to the client to buy the good.

Islamic banks have also been resorting to purchase and resale of properties on a deferred payment basis, which is termed bai' muajjal. It is considered lawful in fiqh (jurisprudence) to charge a higher price for a good if payments are to be made at a later date. According to fiqh, this does not amount to charging interest, since it is not a lending transaction but a trading one. Leasing or ijara is also frequently practiced by Islamic banks.

Under this mode, the banks would buy the equipment or machinery and lease it out to their clients who may opt to buy the items eventually, in which case the monthly payments will consist of two components, i.e., rental for the use of the equipment and instalment towards the purchase price. Reference must also be made to pre-paid purchase of goods, which is termed bai'salam, as a means used by Islamic banks to finance production. Here, the price is paid at the time of the contract but the delivery would take place at a future date. This mode enables an entrepreneur to sell his output to the bank at a price determined in advance. Islamic banks, in keeping with modern times, have extended this facility to manufactures as well.

It is clear from the above sketch that Islamic banking goes beyond the pure financing activities of conventional banks. Islamic banks engage in equity financing and trade financing. By its very nature, Islamic banking is a risky business compared with conventional banking, for risk-sharing forms the very basis of all Islamic financial transactions. To minimize risks, however, Islamic banks have taken pains to distribute the eggs over many baskets and have established reserve funds out of past profits which they can fall back on in the event of any major loss.

3.4 Islamic Banking: Conceptual Framework

Islamic banking transactions and organizations have been growing in the last decade in response to increasing demand. Simultaneously, however, Islamic banks face challenges from non-Islamic institutions because of the mergers of several institutions, inter-organizational collaboration, introduction of new products, improved services, and so on. Other contemporary challenges include continuous environmental change, the speed of change, the impact of the Internet and mobile banking, and the need for an international focus. To respond effectively to these challenges, Islamic financial institutions need to establish management systems that integrate quality management, creativity and innovation. In this context, this chapter deals with conceptual and theoretical framework regards interest free Islamic banking.

3.4.1 Islamic Banking: An Islamic bank is a deposit-taking banking institution whose scope of activities includes all currently known banking activities, excluding borrowing and lending on the basis of interest. On the liabilities side, it mobilizes funds on the basis of a *Mudaraba* or *wakalah* (agent) contract. It can also accept demand deposits which are treated as interest-free loans from the clients to the bank and which are guaranteed. On the assets side, it advances funds on a profit-and-loss sharing or a debt-creating basis, in accordance with the principles of the *Shari'ah*. It plays the role of an investment manager for the owners of time deposits, usually called investment deposits. In addition, equity holding as well as commodity and asset trading constitutes an integral part of Islamic banking operations. An Islamic bank shares its net earnings with its depositors in a way that depends on the size and date to maturity of each deposit. Depositors must be informed beforehand of the formula used for sharing the net earnings with the bank. [15]

3.4.2 Riba: The most salient characteristic of Islamic banking system is the prohibition of *Riba* (often translated as usury or interest), a pre-determined–fixed or variable–charge levied for the use of a loaned commodity; be it real or financial asset. That *riba* is unequivocally banned in Islam is borne by specific references in Islam's holy book, *Qur'an*, and several *ahadith* narrations attributed to Prophet Muhammad. For example, *Qur'an* states, "Believers! Do not consume *riba*, doubling and redoubling... [16], and "...God has made buying and selling lawful and *riba* unlawful..." [17] The common thread running through all such condemnations of *riba* is its exploitative nature and not the concept of profit, which is lawful in Islam if justly and fairly earned.

3.4.3 Mudarabah (Passive Partnership): This is a contract between two parties: a capital owner *(rabb-al-mal)* and an investment manager *(mudarib)*. Profit is distributed between the two parties in accordance with the ratio that they agree upon at the time of the contract. Financial loss is borne by the capital owner; the loss to the manager being the opportunity cost of his own labour, which failed to generate any income for him. Except in the case of a violation of the agreement or default, the investment manager does not guarantee either the capital extended to him or any profit generation. While the provider of capital can impose certain mutually agreed conditions on the manager, he has no right to interfere in the day-to-day work of the manager.

3.4.4 Musharakah (Active Partnership): *A musharakah* contract is similar to that of the *mudaraba,* with the difference that in the case of *musharakah* both partners participate in the management and provision of capital and also share in the profit and loss. Profits are distributed between partners in accordance with agreed ratios, but the loss must be distributed in proportion to the share of each in the total capital.

3.4.5 Diminishing Partnership: This is a contract

between a financier (the bank) and a beneficiary in which the two agree to enter into a partnership to own an asset, but on the condition that the financier will gradually sell his share to the beneficiary at an agreed price and in accordance with an agreed schedule.

3.4.6 Murabahah (Sales Contract at a Profit Mark-Up): Under the *murabahah* contract, the client orders an Islamic bank to purchase for him a certain commodity at a specific cash price, promising to purchase such commodity from the bank once it has been bought, but at a deferred price, which includes an agreed upon profit margin called mark-up in favour of the bank.

3.4.7 Ijara (Leasing): As a form of financing used by Islamic Banks, *Ijara* takes the form of an order by a client to the bank, requesting the bank to purchase a piece of equipment, promising, at the same time, to lease it from the bank after it has been purchased. Thus, this mode of financing includes a purchase order, a promise to lease, and a leasing contract.

3.5 Islamic Banking: An Empirical Framework

It is not possible to cover in this survey all the publications, which have appeared on or Islamic banking. There are numerous publications in Arabic and Urdu, which have made significant contributions to the theoretical discussion. The review of empirical literature pertaining to Islamic banking is discussed below.

Siddiqi (1967) [18] made a pioneering attempt at providing a fairly detailed outline of Islamic banking in Urdu in 1967. (The English version was not published until 1983). His Islamic banking model was based on *mudaraba* and *shirka* (partnership or *musharaka* as it is now usually called). His model was essentially one based on a two-tier *mudaraba* financier-entrepreneur relationship, but he took pains to describe the mechanics of such transactions in considerable detail with numerous hypothetical and arithmetic examples. He classified the operations of an Islamic bank into three categories: services based on fees, commissions or other fixed charges; financing on the basis of *mudaraba* and partnership; and services provided free of charge. His thesis was that such interest-free banks could be a viable alternative to interest-based conventional banks.

Qureshi (1946) [19] looked upon banking as a social service that should be sponsored by the government like public health and education. He took this point of view since the bank could neither pay any interest to account holders nor charge any interest on loans advanced and partnerships between banks and businessmen as a possible alternative, sharing losses if any. No mention was made of profit-sharing.

Ahmad (1952) [20] envisaged the establishment of Islamic banks on the basis of a joint stock company with limited liability. In his scheme, in addition to current accounts, on which no dividend or interest should be paid, there was an account in which people could deposit their capital on the basis of partnership, with shareholders receiving higher dividends than the account holders from the profits made.

Al-Arabi (1966) [21] has versioned a banking system with *mudharaba* as the main pivot. He was actually advancing the idea of a two-tier *mudharaba* which would enable the bank to mobilize savings on a *mudharaba* basis, allocating the funds so mobilized also on a *mudharaba* basis. In his scheme, the bank could advance not only the capital procured through deposits but also the capital of its own shareholders. It is also of interest to note that his position with regard to the distribution of profits and the responsibility for losses was strictly in accordance with the *Shari'ah*.

Irshad (1964) [22] has indicated *mudharaba* as the basis of Islamic banking, but his concept of *mudharaba* was quite different from the traditional one in that he thought of capital and labour (including entrepreneurship) as having equal shares in output, thus sharing the losses and profits equally. This actually means that the owner of capital and the entrepreneur have a fifty-fifty share in the profit or loss as the case may be, which runs counter to the *Shari'ah* position. He envisaged two kinds of deposit accounts. The first sounded like current deposits in the sense that it would be payable on demand, but the money kept in this deposit would be used for social welfare projects, as the depositors would get zero return. The second one amounted to term deposits, which would entitle the depositors to a share in the profits at the end of the year proportionately to the size and duration of the deposits.

He recommended the setting up of a reserve fund, which would absorb all losses so that no depositor would have to bear any loss. According to him, all losses would be either recovered from the reserve fund or borne by the shareholders of the bank.

Chapra (1982) [23] has much concerned about the concentration of economic power which private banks might enjoy in a system based on equity financing. He therefore preferred medium-sized banks, which are neither as large as to wield excessive power nor so small as to be uneconomical. His scheme also contained proposals for loss compensating reserves and loss-absorbing insurance facilities. He also spoke of non-banking financial institutions, which specialize in bringing financiers and entrepreneurs together and act as investment trusts.

Mohsin (1987) [24] has presented a detailed and elaborate framework of Islamic banking in a modern setting. His model incorporates the characteristics of commercial, merchant, and development banks, blending them in a novel fashion. It adds various non-banking services such as trust business, factoring, real estate, and consultancy, as though interest-free banks could not survive by banking business alone. Many of the activities listed certainly go beyond the realm of commercial banking and are so sophisticated and specialized in nature that they may be thought irrelevant to most Muslim countries at their present stage of development. Mohsin's model clearly was designed to fit into a capitalist environment; indeed he explicitly stated that *riba-free* banks could co-exist with interest-based banks.

He envisaged Islamic banks whose nature, outlook and operations could be distinctly different from those of conventional banks. Besides the outlawing of *riba,* he considered it essential that Islamic banks should, since they handle public funds, serve the public interest rather than individual or group interests. In other words, they should play a social-welfare-oriented role rather than a profit-maximizing one. He conceived of Islamic banks as a cross-breed of commercial and merchant banks, investment trusts and investment-management institutions that would offer a wide spectrum of services to their customers. Unlike conventional banks, which depend heavily on the 'crutches of collateral and of non-participation in risk', Islamic banks would have to rely heavily on project evaluation, especially for equity-oriented financing. Thanks to the profit-and-loss sharing nature of the operations, bank-customer relations would be much closer and more cordial than is possible under conventional banking. Finally, the problems of liquidity shortage or surplus would have to be handled differently in Islamic banking, since the ban on interest rules out resort to the money market and the central bank.

Uzair (1978) [25] has suggested adjustments in profit-sharing ratios as a substitute for bank rate manipulations by the central bank. Thus, credit can be tightened by reducing the share accruing to the businessmen and eased by increasing it.

Iqbal and Mirakhor (1987) [26] opines that Islamic banking is a viable proposition that would result in efficient resource allocation. The multi-purpose and extra commercial nature of the Islamic banking operation does not seem to pose intractable problems. The abolition of interest makes it imperative for Islamic banks to look for other instruments, which renders operations outside the periphery of commercial banking unavoidable. Such operations may yield economies of scope. But it is undeniable that the multipurpose character of

Islamic banking poses serious practical problems, especially in relation to the skills needed to handle such diverse and complex transactions.

Naqvi (1978) [27] has pointed out that there is nothing sacrosanct about the institution of *mudharaba* in Islam. He maintains that *mudharaba* is not based on the *Qur'an* or the Hadith but was a custom of the pre-Islamic Arabs. Historically, mudharaba, he contends, enabled the aged, women, and children with capital to engage in trade through merchants for a share in the profit, all losses being borne by the owners of capital, and therefore it cannot claim any sanctity. The fact remains that the Prophet raised no objection to *mudharaba*, so that it was at least not considered un-Islamic. The distribution of profit in *mudharaba* transactions presents practical difficulties, especially where there are multiple providers of capital, but these difficulties are not regarded as insurmountable.

Report of Pakistan's Council of Islamic Ideology (1983) [28] has suggested that the respective capital contributions of parties can be converted to a common denominator by multiplying the amounts provided with the number of days during which each component, such as the firm's own equity capital, its current cash surplus and suppliers' credit was actually deployed in the business, i.e., on a daily product basis. As for deposits, profits (net of administrative expenses, taxes, and appropriation for reserves) would be divided between the shareholders of the bank and the holders of deposits, again on a daily product basis.

Khan's (1986) [29] study showed that these banks had little difficulty in devising practices in conformity with *Shari'ah*. He identified two types of investment accounts: one where the depositor authorized the banks to invest the money in any project and the other where the depositor had a say in the choice of project to be financed. On the asset side, the banks under investigation had been resorting to *mudharaba, musharaka* and *murabaha* modes. Khan's study reported profit rates ranging from 9 to 20 percent, which were competitive with conventional banks in the corresponding areas. The rates of return to depositors varied between 8 and 15 percent, which were quite comparable with the rates of return offered by conventional banks. His study also said that Islamic banks had a preference for trade finance and real estate investments. The study also revealed a strong preference for quick returns, which is understandable in view of the fact that these newly established institutions were anxious to report positive results even in the early years of operation.

Iqbal and Mirakhor (1999) [30] in their study pointed out towards extremely interesting empirical observations, although these were confined to the experience of Iran and Pakistan, both of which attempted to Islamize the entire banking system on a comprehensive basis. Iran switched to Islamic banking in August 1983 with a three-year transition period. The Iranian system allows banks to accept current and savings deposits without having to pay any return, but it permits the banks to offer incentives such as variable prizes or bonus in cash or kind on these deposits. Term deposits (both short-term and long-term) earn a rate of return based on the bank's profits and on the deposit maturity. No empirical evidence is as yet available on the interesting question as to whether interest or a profit-share provides more effective incentive to the depositors for the mobilization of private saving.

Where Islamic and conventional banks existed side by side, central bank control of bank interest rates is liable to be circumvented by shifts of funds to the Islamic banks. This study also noted that the conversion to Islamic modes has been much slower on the asset than on the deposit side. It appears that the Islamic banking system in Iran was able to use less than half of its resources for credit to the private sector, mostly in the form of short-term facilities, i.e., commercial and trade transactions. The slower pace of conversion on the asset side was attributed by the authors to the inadequate supply of personnel trained in long-term financing. The authors, however, found no evidence to show that the effectiveness of monetary policy in Iran, broadly speaking, was altered by the conversion.

Therefore, this study expressed considerable uneasiness about the concentration of bank assets on short-term trade credits rather than on long-term financing. This the authors found undesirable, not only because it is inconsistent with the intentions of the new system, but also because the heavy concentration on a few assets might increase risks and destabilize the asset portfolios. The study also drew attention to the difficulty experienced in both Iran and Pakistan in financing budget deficits under a non-interest system and underscored the urgent need to devise suitable interest-free instruments. Iran has, however, decreed that government borrowing on the basis of a fixed rate of return from the nationalized banking system would not amount to interest and would hence be permissible. The official rationalization is that, since all banks are nationalized, interest rates and payments among banks will cancel out in the consolidated accounts.

Haq Nadeem ul and Mirakhor, Abbas (1987) [31] in their study revealed that current accounts in all cases are operated on the principles of *al-wadiah*. Savings deposits, too, are accepted on the basis of *al-wadiah*, but 'gifts' to depositors are given entirely at the discretion of the Islamic banks on the minimum balance, so that the depositors also share in profits. Investment deposits are invariably based on the *mudaraba* principle, but there are considerable variations. Thus, for example, the Islamic Bank of Bangladesh has been offering PLS Deposit Accounts, PLS Special Notice Deposit Accounts, and PLS Term Deposit Accounts, while Bank Islam Malaysia has been operating two kinds of investment deposits, one for the general public and the other for institutional clients. Their studies also show that the profit-sharing ratios and the modes of payment vary from place to place and from time to time. Thus, for example, profits are provisionally declared on a monthly basis in Malaysia, on a quarterly basis in Egypt, on a half-yearly basis in Bangladesh and Pakistan, and on an annual basis in Sudan.

A striking common feature of all these banks is that even their investment deposits are mostly short-term, reflecting the depositors' preference for assets in as liquid form as far as possible. Even in Malaysia, where investment deposits have accounted for a much larger proportion of the total, the bulk of them were made for a period of less than two years. By contrast, in Sudan most of the deposits have consisted of current and savings deposits, apparently because of the ceiling imposed by the Sudanese monetary authorities on investment deposits, which in turn was influenced by limited investment opportunities in the domestic economy. There are also interesting variations in the pattern of resource utilization by the Islamic banks.

For example, *musharaka* has been far more important than *murabaha* as an investment mode in Sudan, while the reverse has been the case in Malaysia. On the average, however, *murabaha, bai'muajjal* and *ijara*, rather than *musharaka* represent the most commonly used modes of financing. The case studies also show that the structure of the clientele has been skewed in favour of the more affluent segment of society, no doubt because the banks are located mainly in metropolitan centres with small branch networks.

The two main problems identified by the case studies are the absence of suitable non-interest based financial instruments for money and capital market transactions and the high rate of borrower delinquency. The former problem has been partially redressed by Islamic banks resorting to mutual inter-bank arrangements and central bank cooperation, as mentioned earlier. The Bank Islam Malaysia, for instance, has been placing its excess liquidity with the central bank, which usually exercises its discretionary powers to give some returns. The delinquency problem appears to be real and serious.

Murabaha payments have often been held up because late payments cannot be penalized, in contrast to the interest system in which delayed payments would automatically mean increased interest payments. To overcome this problem, the Pakistani banks have resorted to what is called 'mark-down' which is the opposite of 'mark-up' (i.e., the profit margin in the cost-plus approach of *Murabaha* transactions). 'Mark-down' amounts to giving rebates as an incentive for early payments. But the legitimacy of this 'mark-down' practice is questionable on *Shari'ah* grounds, since it is time-based and therefore smacks of interest.

In the Southeast Asian context, two studies conducted by Zakariah Man (1988) and Mastura (1988) [32] have revealed that the Malaysian experience in Islamic banking has been encouraging. Man's study shows that the average return to depositors has been quite competitive with that offered by conventional banks. By the end of 1986, after three years of operation, the bank had a network of fourteen branches. However, 90 percent of its deposits had maturities of two years or less, and non-Muslim depositors accounted for only 2 percent of the total. Man is particularly critical of the fact that the *mudaraba* and *musharaka* modes of operation, which are considered most meaningful by Islamic scholars, accounted for a very small proportion of the total investment portfolio, while *bai'muajjal* and *ijara* formed the bulk of the total.

It is evident from Mastura's analysis that the Philippine Amanah Bank is, strictly speaking, not an Islamic bank, as interest-based operations continue to co-exist with Islamic modes of financing. Thus, the PAB has been operating both interest and Islamic 'windows' for deposits. Mastura's study has produced evidence to show that the PAB has been concentrating on *murabaha* transactions, paying hardly any attention to the *mudaraba* and *musharaka* means of financing. The PAB has also been adopting unorthodox approaches in dealing with excess liquidity by making use of interest-bearing treasury bills. Nonetheless, the PAB has also been invoking some Islamic modes in several major investment activities. Mastura has made special references to the *qirad* principle adopted by the PAB in the Kilu-sang Kabuhayan at Kaunlaran (KKK) movement launched under Marcos and to the *ijara* financing for the acquisition of farm implements and supplies in the Quedon food production program undertaken by the present regime.

Nien-haus (1988) [33] concluded that Islamic banking is viable at microeconomic level but dismisses the proponents' ideological claims for superiority of Islamic banking as 'unfounded'. He also pointed out that there are some failure stories. Examples cited include the Kuwait Finance House which had its fingers burnt by investing heavily in the Kuwaiti real estate and construction sector in 1984, and the Islamic Bank International of Denmark which suffered heavy losses in 1985 and 1986 to the tune of more than 30 percent of its paid-up capital. But then, as he has also noted, that the quoted troubles of individual banks had specific causes and it would be inappropriate to draw general conclusions from particular cases. He also noted that the high growth rates of the initial years have been falling off, but he rejects the thesis that Islamic banks have reached their 'limits of growth' after filling a market gap. The falling growth rates might well be due to the bigger base values, and the growth performance of Islamic banks has been relatively better in most cases than that of conventional banks in recent years.

3.6 Conclusion

It could be concluded from above conceptual and empirical discussion that Islamic banking is not a negligible or merely a temporary phenomenon. Islamic banks are here to stay and there are signs that they will continue to grow and expand. Even if one does not subscribe to the Islamic injunction against the institution of interest, one may find in Islamic banking some innovative ideas which could add more variety to the existing financial network. One of the main selling points of Islamic banking, at least in theory, is that, unlike conventional banking, it is concerned about the viability of the project and the profitability of the operation but not the size of the collateral.

Good projects which might be turned down by conventional banks for lack of collateral would be financed by Islamic banks on a profit-sharing basis. It is especially in this sense that Islamic banks can play a catalytic role in stimulating economic development. In many developing countries, of course, development banks are supposed to perform this function. Islamic banks are expected to be more enterprising than their conventional counterparts. In practice, however, Islamic banks have been concentrating on short-term trade finance which is the least risky.

Part of the explanation is that long-term financing requires expertise which is not always available. Another reason is that there are no back-up institutional structures such as secondary capital markets for Islamic financial instruments. It is possible also that the tendency to concentrate on short-term financing reflects the early years of operation: it is easier to administer, less risky, and the returns are quicker. The banks may learn to pay more attention to equity financing as they grow older. It is sometimes suggested that Islamic banks are rather complacent. They tend to behave as though they had a captive market in the Muslim masses that will come to them on religious grounds. This complacency seems more pronounced in countries with only one Islamic bank.

Many Muslims find it more convenient to deal with conventional banks and have no qualms about shifting their deposits between Islamic banks and conventional ones depending on which bank offers a better return. This might suggest a case for more Islamic banks in those countries as it would force the banks to be more innovative and competitive. Another solution would be to allow the conventional banks to undertake equity financing and/or to operate Islamic 'counters' or 'windows', subject to strict compliance with the *Shari'ah* rules. It is perhaps not too wild a proposition to suggest that there is a need for specialized Islamic financial institutions such as mudaraba banks, murabaha banks and musharaka banks which would compete with one another to provide the best possible services.

End Notes

1. Islamic Financial Institutions (outside Pakistan and Iran): *The list includes Islamic banks as well as Islamic investment companies but it does not include Islamic insurance or takaful companies.* Australia Islamic Investment Company, Melbourne; Bahamas Dar al Mal al Islami, Nassau Islamic Investment Company Ltd, Nassau, Masraf Faisal Islamic Bank and Trust, Bahamas Ltd; Bahrain Albaraka Islamic Investment Bank, Manama, Bahrain Islamic Bank, Manama, Bahrain Islamic Investment Company, Manama, Islamic Investment Company of the Gulf, Masraf Faisal al Islami, Bahrain.; Bangladesh Islamic Bank of Bangladesh Ltd, Dhaka; Denmark Islamic Bank International of Denmark, Copenhagen; Egypt Albaraka Nile Valley Company, Cairo, Arab Investment Bank (Islamic Banking Operations), Cairo., Bank Misr (Islamic Branches), Cairo, Faisal Islamic Bank of Egypt, Cairo, General Investment Company, Cairo, Islamic International Bank for Investment and Development, Cairo, Islamic Investment and Development Company, Cairo, Nasir Social Bank, Cairo; Guinea Islamic Investment Company of Guinea, Conakry, Masraf Faisal al Islami of Guinea, Conakry; India Baitun Nasr Urban Cooperative Society, Bombay; Jordan Islamic Investment House Company Ltd Amman, Jordan Finance House, Amman, Jordan Islamic Bank for Finance and Investment, Amman; Kibris (Turkish Cyprus) Faisal Islamic Bank of Kibris, Lefkosa; Kuwait Al Tukhaim International Exchange Company, Safat., Kuwait Finance House, Safat; Liberia African Arabian Islamic Bank, Monrovia; Liechtenstein Arinco Arab Investment Company, Vaduz, Islamic Banking System Finance S.A. Vaduz; Luxembourg Islamic Finance House Universal Holding S.A; Malaysia Bank Islam Malaysia Berhad, Kuala Lumpur, Pilgrims Management and Fund Board, Kuala Lumpur; Mauritania Albaraka Islamic Bank, Mauritania; Niger Faisal Islamic Bank of Niger, Niamy; Philippines Philippine Amanah Bank, Zamboanga; Qatar Islamic Exchange and Investment Company, Doha, Qatar Islamic Bank; Saudi Arabia Albaraka Investment

and Development Company, Jeddah, Islamic Development Bank, Jeddah; Senegal Faisal Islamic Bank of Senegal, Dakar, Islamic Investment Company of Senegal, Dakar; South Africa JAAME Ltd., Durban; Sudan Bank al Baraka al Sudani, Khartoum, Faisal Islamic Bank of Sudan, Khartoum, Islamic Bank of Western Sudan, Khartoum, Islamic Cooperative Development Bank, Khartoum, Islamic Investment Company of Sudan, Khartoum, Sudan Islamic Bank, Khartoum, Tadamun Islamic Bank, Khartoum, Jersey The Islamic Investment Company, St Helier, Masraf Faisal al Islami, St Helier ;Switzerland Dar al Mal al Islami, Geneva., Islamic Investment Company Ltd, Geneva, Shariah Investment Services, PIG, Geneva; Thailand Arabian Thai Investment Company Ltd, Bangkok; Tunisia Bank al Tamwil al Saudi al Tunisi; Turkey Albaraka Turkish Finance House, Istanbul, Faisal Finance Institution, Istanbul; U.A.E. Dubai Islamic Bank, Dubai, Islamic Investment Company Ltd, Sharjah; U.K. Albaraka International Ltd, London, Albaraka Investment Co. Ltd, London, Al Rajhi Company for Islamic Investment Ltd, London, Islamic Finance House Public Ltd Co., London.

2. Ready, R.K. (1981), "The March Towards Self-determination", paper presented at the First Advanced Course on Islamic Banks, International Institute of Islamic Banking and Economics, Cairo, 28 August-17 September.

3. Siddiqi, M.N. (1988), "Islamic Banking: Theory and Practice", in M. Ariff (ed.), (1982), "Monetary Policy in an Interest-free Islamic Economy-Nature and Scope", in M. Ariff, (ed.), Monetary and Fiscal Economics of Islam, International Centre for Research in Islamic Economics, Jeddah.

4. Mastura, Michael O. (1988), "Islamic Banking: The Philippine Experience", in M. Ariff (ed.), (1982), "Monetary Policy in an Interest-free Islamic Economy-Nature and Scope", in M. Ariff, (ed.), Monetary and Fiscal Economics of Islam, International Centre for Research in Islamic Economics, Jeddah.

5. Man, Zakariya (1988), "Islamic Banking: The Malaysian Experience", in M. Ariff (ed.), (1982), "Monetary Policy in an Interest-free Islamic Economy-Nature and Scope", in M. Ariff, (ed.), Monetary and Fiscal Economics of Islam, International Centre for Research in Islamic Economics, Jeddah.

6. Chapra, M. Umer (1982), 'Money and Banking in an Islamic

Economy" in M. Ariff (ed.), (1982), "Monetary Policy in an Interest-free Islamic Economy-Nature and Scope", in M. Ariff, (ed.), Monetary and Fiscal Economics of Islam, International Centre for Research in Islamic Economics, Jeddah.

7. Surah al-Rum (Chapter 30), verse 39; Surah al-Nisa (Chapter 39), verse 161; Surah al-Imran (Chapter 3), verses 130-2; Surah al-Baqarah (Chapter 2), verses 275-81. See Yusuf Ali's Translation of the Qur'an.

8. Hadith compiled by Muslims (Kitab al-Musaqat).

9. Khan, Muhammad Akram (1968), "Theory of Employment in Islam", Islamic Literature, Karachi, XIV(4): 5-16.

10. Ariff, M. (1982), "Monetary Policy in an Interest-free Islamic Economy-Nature and Scope", in M. Ariff, (ed.), Monetary and Fiscal Economics of Islam, International Centre for Research in Islamic Economics, Jeddah.

11. This refers to a Hadith compiled by Muslims (Kitab al-Musaqat).

12. Kahf, Monzer, (1982a), "Saving and investment functions in a Two-sector Islamic Economy", in M. Ariff (ed.), (1982), Monetary and Fiscal Economics of Islam, International Centre for Research in Islamic Economics, Jeddah.

13. Bank Islam Malaysia Berhad has been offering a 70:30 profit-sharing ratio in favour of depositors (Man, 1988).

14. In 1984 the Islamic Bank of Bangladesh offered rates of return ranging from 4.95 percent to 14.13 percent. The Faisal Islamic Bank of Egypt, Cairo, gave a 9 percent rate of return on deposits in the same year (Afkar Inquiry, December 1985).

15. Mabid Ali Al-Jarhi and Munawar Iqbal (2001), Islamic Banking: Answers to Some Frequently Asked Questions, Occasional Paper 4, Islamic Research and Training Institute, Jeddah, p. 21.

16. Holy Qur'an Chapter. 3, verse 130.

17. Holy Qur'an Chapter. 2, verse 274.

18. Siddiqi, M. Nejatullah (1967), Banking Without Interest (Urdu), Lahore: Islamic Publications, Revised Version (1983).

19. Qureshi, Anvar Iqbal (1946), Islam and Theory of Interest, Sh. M. Asraf, Lahore, pp. 64-67.

20. Sheikh Mahmud Ahmad (1952), Economics of Islam, Lahore, Ch. VII.

21. Mohammad Abdullah Al-Arabi, (1966), "Contemporary Banking Transactions and Islam's Views There On", Islamic

Review, London, May, p. 1016.

22. Irshad S.A. (1964), Interest-free Banking, Orient Press of Pakistan, Karachi, pp. 28-40.

23. M. Umer Chapra (1982), 'Money and Banking in an Islamic Economy in M. Ariff (ed.), (1982), Monetary and Fiscal Economics of Islam, International Centre for Research in Islamic Economics, Jeddah.

24. Mohsin Khan (1987), "Principles of Islamic Monetary Theory and Policy" paper presented at seminar on Islamic Economics for University Teachers, Islamabad, Pakistan, pp. 12-24.

25. Uzair, Mohamed, (1978), Interest-free Banking, Royal Book, Co., Karachi, Pakistan, pp. 4-12.

26. Zamir Iqbal and Abbas Mirakhor (1987), Islamic Banking, International Monetary Fund, Occasional Paper 49, Washington D.C.

27. Naqvi, S.N.H. (1978), Ethical Foundations of Islamic Economics, Journal of Islamic Economics, Journal of Islamic Studies, Summer.

28. Council of Islamic Ideology, Pakistan (1981), The Elimination of Interest from the Economy of Pakistan, Council of Islamic Ideology, Islamabad.

29. Khan, M.S. (1986), Islamic Interest-free Banking: A Theoretical Analysis, International Monetary Fund Staff Papers, No. 33, pp. 1-27.

30. Iqbal, Zamir and Abbas Mirakhor (1999), "Progress and Challenges of Islamic Banking", Thunderbird International Business Review, Vol. 41, No. 4/5, pp. 381-405.

31. Haq, Nadeem Ul, and Mirakhor, Abbas (1987), "Saving Behaviour in an Economy without Fixed Interest." Theoretical Studies in Islamic Banking and Finance; Khan, Mohsin S. and Mirakhor, Abbas, (eds.): The Institute for Research and Islamic Studies, Houston, Texas, United States, pp. 125-40.

32. Zakariya Man (1988), "Islamic Banking: The Malaysian Experience", in M. Arif, Islamic Banking, Asian Pacific Economic Literature, Vol. 2, No. 2, pp. 48-64.

33. Nien-haus, V. (1988), Profitability of Islamic PLS Banks competing with Interest Banks: Problems and Prospects, Journal of Research in Islamic Economics, 1(1); p. 3747.

4

Islamic Financial Institutions/Banks:
A Global View

4.1 Introduction
During the past thirty five years a number of Islamic financial institutions have been established in different Muslim as well as in some non-Muslim countries. These include Islamic banks, Islamic investment companies and Islamic insurance and re-insurance companies. The basic motivation for the establishment of these institutions is the desire of Muslims to reorganize their financial activities in such a way, which shall not violate any canons of Islamic *Shari'ah* in general and will enable them to conduct their financial activities without indulging in *Riba* in particular. [1] The purpose of this part of the analysis is to present a survey of Islamic banking scene and describes some of the major techniques used by Islamic banks.

4.2 Performance of Islamic Financial Institutions (IFIs)
The contemporary Islamic banking scene essentially consists of three different and independent elements [2]:
1. Islamic banks and Islamic financial institutions (IFIs) in different parts of the world which have been in some 38 countries including Europe, United States, the Far East, South Asia and the Middle East during the past thirty five years or so.
2. Countries where attempts have been undertaken to restructure the whole banking system along the Islamic lines.
3. Islamic credit societies which exist in the unorganized banking sector in several countries.
    However, this part of the analysis is mainly concerned

with the financial institutions, which mostly belong to the first category, although occasionally some reference may also be made about the financial institutions in other two categories.

4.2.1 Number of Islamic Financial Institutions: The set of Islamic financial institutions in the world would include all the institutions mentioned in the above three categories. However, the number of institutions in some of these categories is not known exactly. Nevertheless, it is possible to make some reasonable and educated guess. Keeping in view the fact that all commercial banks in at least three countries, viz. Iran, Pakistan and Sudan are required to conduct their activities in accordance with the Islamic principles and also including the Islamic financial institutions operating in the unorganized sector in some Muslim as well as non-Muslim countries, the total number of institutions which adhere to Islamic principles and could be described IFIs may be close to a thousand. However, due to lack of reliable information, it is preferable to confine this part of the analysis only to Islamic institutions operating in the organized private sector.

Table 4.1 describes the list of Islamic banks and Islamic financial institutions.

Table 4.1: List of Islamic Banks and Islamic Financial Institutions

S.N	Country	Name of Islamic Bank or Financial Institution	Year of establishment
1.	Albania	United Bank of Albania	1992
2.	Algeria	Banque Al-Baraka D'Algerie	1991
3.	Australia [3]	Muslim Community Cooperative	1989
4.	Azerbaizan	Kauthar Bank	1992
5.	Bahrain [4]	ABC Islamic Bank	1985
6.		Al Amin Bank	1987
7.		Al-Barakah Islamic Bank	1984
8.		Bahrain Islamic Bank, B.S.C.	1979
9.		Gulf Finance House (BSC) E.C.	1999
10.		Investors Bank	1997
11.		Kuwait Finance House (Bahrain) B.S.C.	2002

Contd...

12.		Shamil Bank of Bahrain B.S.C.	2000
13.	Bangladesh [5]	Islami Bank Bangladesh Ltd.	1983
14.		Shahjalal Islami Bank Ltd.	2000
15.		Social Investment Bank Ltd.	1995
16.	Bosnia Herzegovina	Bosnia Bank International	2000
17.	Brunei	Islamic Development Bank of Brunei Bhd	2000
18.		The Islamic Bank of Brunei Bhd	1992
19.	Egypt	Egyptian Saudi Finance Bank	1988
20.		Faisal Islamic Bank of Egypt	1977
21.		Islamic International Bank for Investment and Development	1980
22.	Gambia	Arab Gambian Islamic Bank Ltd.	1994
23.	Guinea	Banque Islamique de Guinee	
24.	Indonesia [6]	PT Bank Syariah Mandiri	1999
25.		PT. Bank Syariah Mualmalat	1992
26.	Iran	Bank Keshavarzi (Agriculture)	1980
27.		Bank Mellat	1980
28.		Bank Melli Iran	1927
29.		Bank of Maskan	1937
30.		Bank Refah	1960
31.		Bank Saderat Iran	1952
32.		Bank Sanat Va Madan	1979
33.		Bank Sepah	1925
34.		Bank Tejarat	1980
35.		Eqtesad Novid	2001
36.		Export Development Bank of Iran	1991
37.		Karafarin Bank	1999
38.		Parsian Bank	2001
39.		Saman Bank	1999
40.	Iraq	Kurdistan Intl' Bank for Investment & Development	2005
41.	Jordan	Beit Al-Mal Saving &Investment Co.	1983
42.		Islamic Intl Arab Bank plc	1998
43.		Jordan Islamic Bank	1978
44.	Kuwait	Al Madar Finance & Investment	1998
45.		Aref Investment Group	1975
46.		First Investment	1997
47.		Gulf Investment House	1998
48.		International Investment Group	1988
49.		Investment Dar	1994
50.		Kuwait Finance House	1977
51.		Osoul Leasing & Finance	1999
52.		The International Investor	1992

Contd...

No.	Country	Name	Year
53.		The International Leasing and Investment Co.	1999
54.		The Securities House	2003
55.	Lebanon [7]	Al Baraka Bank Lebanon	1991
56.	Malaysia	Bank Islam Malysia Berhad	1983
57.		Bank Muamalat	1999
58.		RHB Islamic Bank	2005
59.	Mauritania	Banque Al Wava Mauritanienne Islamique	1985
60.	Niger	Banque Islamique du Niger pour le Commerce et l'Investissement	
61.	Pakistan	Al Zamin Leasing Modaraba	1992
62.		B.F. Modaraba	1989
63.		B.R.R. International Modaraba	1985
64.		Faysal Bank Limited	1994
65.		Fayzan Manufacturing Modaraba	2001
66.		First Allied Bank Modaraba	1993
67.		First Elite Capital Modaraba	1991
68.		First Equity Modaraba	1992
69.		First Fidelity Leasing Modaraba	1991
70.		First General Leasing Modaraba	1991
71.		First Habib Bank Modaraba	1991
72.		First Habib Modaraba	1985
73.		First IBL Modaraba	1990
74.		First Imrooz Modaraba	1994
75.		First Mehran Modaraba	1990
76.		First National Modaraba	1989
77.		First Pak Modaraba	1991
78.		First Paramount Modaraba	1995
79.		First Prudential Modaraba	1989
80.		First Punjab Modaraba	1993
81.		First Standard Investment Bank Ltd	2002
82.		First UDL Modarba	1991
83.		Guardian Modaraba	1991
84.		LTV Capital Modaraba	1987
85.		Meezan Bank Ltd.	1997
86.		Modaraba Al- Mali	1987
87.		Modaraba Al-Tijarah	1991
88.		Standard Chartered Modaraba	1987
89.		Trust Modaraba	1991
90.		Unity Modaraba	1994
91.	Palestine [8]	Arab Islamic Bank	1995
92.		Palestine Islamic Bank	1995
93.	Philippines	Al Amanah Islamic Inv. Bank of the Philippines	1990
94.	Qatar [9]	First Finance	1999

Contd...

95.		International Islamic	1990
96.		Qatar Islamic Bank	1982
97.	Russia	Badr-Forte Bank	1998
98.	Saudi Arabia	Al Rajhi Bank	1987
99.		Al Tawfeek Co. for Investment Funds	1992
100.		Bank Al-Jazira	1975
101.	Senegal	Banque Islamique Du Senegal	1983
102.	South Africa	Al Baraka Bank Ltd.	1989
103.		Oasis Group Holdings (PTY) Ltd.	1996
104.	Sudan	Agricultural Bank of Sudan	1957
105.		Al Baraka Bank–Sudan	1984
106.		Al Shamal Islamic Bank	1985
107.		Al Tadamon Islamic Bank	1981
108.		Animal Resources Bank	1992
109.		Bank of Khartoum	1913
110.		Blue Nile Mashreq Bank	1983
111.		El-Nilein Industrial Development	1993
112.		Export Development Bank	1984
113.		Faisal Islamic Bank–Sudan	1977
114.		Farmers' Commercial Bank	1999
115.		Financial Investment Bank	1997
116.		Gedarif Investment Bank	1995
117.		Habib Bank Ltd.	1982
118.		Islamic Cooperative Development Bank	1983
119.		Industrial Development Bank	
120.		Ivory Bank	
121.		National Bank of Abu Dhabi	
122.		National Bank of Sudan	1981
123.		Omdurman National Bank	1993
124.		Saudi Sudanese Bank	1984
125.		Savings & Social Development Bank	1995
126.		Sudanese French Bank	1978
127.		Sudanese Islamic Bank	1982
128.		The Commercial & Real Estate Bank	1966
129.		Worker' National Bank	1987
130.	Switzerland	Faisal Finace (Swiss) S.A.	1980
131.	Thailand	The Islamic Bank of Thailand	2002
132.	Tunisia	Beit Ettamwil Saoudi Tounsi (Best Bank)	1983
133.		Tunisie Saudi Financial Leasing House	
134.	Turkey	Al Baraka Turkish Finance House	1984
135.		Anadolu Finans Kurumu A.S.	1991
136.		Asya Finans Kurumu A.S.	1996
137.		Family Finance Kurumu A.S.	
138.		Kuwait Turkish Evkaf Finance House	1988

Contd...

139.	United Arab Emirates	Abu Dhabi Islamic Bank	1997
140.		Amlak Finance PJSC	2000
141.		Dubai Islamic Bank	1975
142.		HSBC Amanah	1998
143.		Emirates Islamic Bank	2004
144.		Sharjah Islamic Bank	2002
145.	United Kingdom	Islamic Bank of Britain Plc	2004
146.		European Islamic Investment Bank Plc	2006
147.	United States	Lariba American Finance House	1987
148.	Yemen	Islamic Bank of Yemen for Finance & Investment	1995
149.		Saba Islamic Bank	1997
150.		Shamil Bank of Yemen & Bahrain	2002
151.		Tadhamon Intl Islamic Bank	1995

Source: Islamic Finance Directory, General Counsel for Islamic Banks and Financial Institutions, Bahrain.

The list of 151 Islamic financial institutions operating in different parts of the world, along with their year of establishment, includes Islamic banks, Islamic investment companies and Islamic insurance companies. However, the actual number of Islamic financial institutions in the organized private sector may be much more than this. In fact, certain observers of the Islamic banking scene believe that total number of such institutions may not be less than 400 managing assets of US$ 1 trillion globally. However, reliable information is not available on all of them. Hence, the list supplied in above table may be accepted only as a work list of these institutions. It should also be noted that some of the Banks mentioned in the table have been established as early as 1930. However, these Banks started to function as conventional banks and were converted to Islamic banks after the process of Islamisation of the banking sector in Pakistan, Sudan and Iran. Table 4.2 describes global summary of Islamic banking.

A global summary of the financial highlights of 116 Islamic banks and financial institutions is discussed below. Islamic banks and financial institutions (IFIs) have become an integral part of the international finance and the regional banking industry. Clearly shown through its widespread and growth, size since the 1970s, the Islamic Financial Service Industry (IFSI) has developed from being individual trials into an integrated industry with its own basics, standards, criteria, products and institutions.

The total assets of Islamic banks and financial institutions witnessed an annual growth rate of 23 percent during 1993-2003. This resulted in the rise of total assets from US$ 53.3 billion in 1993 to US$ 175 billion in 2003. This was after IFSI reached its peak in 2001 with US$ 269 billion and then decreased to US$ 147.3 billion due to the devaluation in the Iranian currency against the US dollar in 2002 when IFSI assets decreased by 44 percent.

Table 4.2: Global Summary of Islamic Banking

(US$ 000's)

Financial Highlights	2001	2002	2003
Paid-up Capital	13,843,642	7,428,056	7,308,540
Total Equity	16,928,583	13,359,810	15,006,320
Total Assets	269,027,886	144,821,894	174,715,040
Cash and Cash equivalents	54,649,696	25,295,033	27,593,628
Contra Accounts	45,674,084	34,282,903	38,188,051
Total Investments	185,164,105	108,032,424	134,283,098
Total Deposits	222,014,349	118,093,460	137,506,930
Current Accounts and Savings	100,964,379	48,247,477	56,381,774
Restricted Investment Account	5,878,301	4,614,069	4,761,876
Unrestricted Investment Account	111,450,340	66,381,437	77,418,426
Reserves	2,767,882	3,275,271	3,890,338
Net Profit	2,446,202	1,797,794	2,736,388

Source: Computed.

4.2.2 Geographical Spread of Islamic Financial Institutions: Islamic financial institutions are not confined to any specific geographical region. They are located in the Arab world as well as in the non-Arab world. There are IFIs in the capital surplus economies as well as in the labour surplus economies. They are working in the developing countries as well as in the advanced industrial countries. Thus, it could be said that IFIs, despite their small number, are spatially well diversified.

As regards the IFIs functioning in Muslim countries, 163 are located in 26 Muslim countries. Pakistan has the maximum number (30) of IFIs, followed by Sudan (26) and Bahrain (21). It is significant to note that in the Indian sub- continent alone, there are 39 IFIs (Pakistan 30 and Bangladesh 9) which is nearly one-fourth of the total IFIs. It is also notable that nearly 60 IFIs are located in the non-Arab world. There are 18 Islamic financial institutions which are functioning in 10 different non-Muslim countries, such as Australia, Philippines, South Africa, Switzerland and United Kingdom.

4.2.3 Progress in the Establishment of IFIs: The first attempt to establish an Islamic financial institution took place in Pakistan in the late 1950s with the establishment of a local Islamic bank in a rural area. [10] Some pious landlords who deposited funds at no interest, and then loaned to small landowners for agricultural development initiated the experiment. The borrower did not pay interest on the credit advanced, but a small charge was levied to cover the bank's operational expenses. The charge was far lower than the rate of interest. Although the experience was encouraging, two main factors were responsible for its failure. First, the depositor landlords regarded the deposits as a one-time event. With the increasing number of borrowers, the gap between available capital and credit demanded was huge. Secondly, the bank staff did not have complete autonomy over its operation; depositors showed considerable interest in the way their money was lent out.

In terms of historical evolution of IFIs, mention should also be made of a unique financial institution which is generally not mentioned in the discussions of Islamic banking but whose significance, importance cannot be ignored. It is the "Pilgrims Management and Fund Board" of Malaysia which is popularly known as Tabung Haji. The reason for the establishment of this institution was the desire of Malaysian Muslims that money spent on the pilgrimage (Haj) must be clean and untainted with Riba. Since this was not possible by putting the money with the ordinary commercial banks, this desire led to the establishment of a special financial institution. Consequently, "Pilgrims Saving Corporation" was established in 1963 which was later incorporated into the "Pilgrims Management and Fund Board" (Tabung Haji) in 1969. [11] Another pioneering experiment of putting the principles of Islamic banking and finance into practice was conducted in Mit-Ghamr in Egypt from 1963 to 1967.

The pioneering effort led by Ahmad El Najjar, took the form of a savings bank based on profit sharing in the Egyptian town of Mit Ghamr in 1963. [12] The experiment combined the idea of German saving banks with the principles of rural banking within the general framework of Islamic values. The bank's operation was based on the same Islamic principle i.e. no interest to the depositors or from the borrowers. Unlike the Pakistani bank mentioned earlier, the borrower had to have deposits in the bank in order to request a loan. The experiment soon became successful; more branches were opened in different parts of the country, and the amount of deposits increased. Hence, what started as a single bank operation expanded to form a network of local savings banks. Although the project made a good start and initial results were more than encouraging, it suffered a setback owing to changes in the political atmosphere. Nevertheless, the project was revived in 1971 under the name of Nasser Social Bank. This was the first Islamic bank in an urban setting based in Cairo.

The bank is a public authority with an autonomous status.

Its purpose was mainly to promote social concerns such as granting of interest-free loans for small projects on a profit-loss sharing basis, and assistance to the poor and needy students for university and higher education. Because of these social functions, Nasser Social Bank was granted an exemption from the Banking and Credit Law of 1957 in its initial stages. The Bank originated under the Ministry of Treasury but it is now functioning under the Ministry of Social Welfare and Insurance. It's capital comes from the funds allocated by the President from extra budgetary resources, appropriation from the state budget, and contribution from the Ministry of Awqaf. The principles of operation of the Nasser Social Bank are very similar to those of the Mit Ghamr Savings Bank. However, the latter offers a full range of normal banking services and a wide range of investment activities through equity participation. [13]

Next to follow was the Dubai Islamic Bank in 1975. The Dubai Islamic Bank is a public limited company having its head office at Dubai, United Arab Emirates, with a capital of US$ 272 billion. Since then a number of Islamic banks and Islamic financial institutions have been established in different parts of the world and are functioning successfully. A significant development in Islamic banking has been the granting of an Islamic bank license in Saudi Arabia to the fifty-year old "Al-Rajhi Company", a firm noted for its currency, exchange and commercial activities, whose assets exceed US$ 5 billion. The firm started operation in 1985 under the name of "Al-Rajhi Banking Investment Corporation" and has since developed active relationships with major manufacturing and trading companies in Europe and several US corporations.

The progress in the establishment of Islamic financial institutions shows that movement of establishing Islamic financial institutions started in the second half of seventies and reached its peak in the middle eighties. By the end of 1980, there were 20 Islamic financial institutions working in different parts of the world. During the next decade (1981-1990), the number of IFIs increased three fold and 60 new institutions came into being. This is because of the Islamisation of the financial system of Pakistan, Sudan and Iran. This pace continued in the next 10 years also and another 60 new IFIs were established during 1991-2000. Table 4.3 describes the progress in the establishment of Islamic banks/Islamic financial institutions.

Table 4.3: Progress in the Establishment of Islamic Banks/Islamic Financial Institutions

Year	No. of Institutions established during the year	Name of Islamic Banks/IFIs
1963	1	Pilgrims Management and Fund Board of Malaysia (Tabung Haji)
1971	1	Nasser Social Bank
1975	4	Islamic Development Bank, Jeddah Dubai Islamic Bank UAE, Aref Investment Group, Kuwait, Bank Al Jazira, Saudi Arabia
1977	3	Faisal Islamic Bank, Egypt; Kuwait Finance House, Kuwait; Faisal Islamic Bank, Sudan
1978	2	Jordan Islamic Bank, Jordan; Sudanese French Bank, Sudan
1979	3	Bahrain Islamic Bank; National Investment Trust, Pakistan, Bank Sanat Va Madan, Iran
1980	6	Islamic International Bank for Investment and Development, Egypt; Arab Insurance Company, U.A.E, Bank Kesavarzi, Iran, Bank Mellat, Iran, Bank Tejarat, Iran, Faisal Finace (Swiss) S.A, Switzerland
1981	5	Islamic Investment Company, Bahrain Islamic Finance House Company, Jordan Banker's Equity Limited, Pakistan, Al Tadamon Islamic Bank, Sudan, National Bank of Sudan
1982	3	Philippine Amanah Bank; Qatar Islamic Bank, Qatar, Sudanese Islamic Bank, Sudan

Contd...

1983	11	Faisal Islamic Bank, Bahrain; Islamic Bank (Bangladesh) Limited, Bangladesh; Islamic Bank International, Denmark; Bank Islam Malaysia Berhad; Islamic Investment Company, Qatar; Islamic Bank for Western Sudan; Islamic Cooperative Development, Sudan; Al Baraka Islamic Bank, Sudan Sudanese Islamic Bank, Sudan, Beit Al-Mal Saving &Investment Co, Jordan, Banque Islamique Du Senegal, Beit Ettamwil Saoudi Tounsi (Best Bank), Tunisia
1984	16	Al-Barakah Investment and Development Company, Saudi Arabia; Al Baraka Islamic Bank, Bahrain; Faisal Islamic Bank, Guinea Islamic Investment Company, Guinea Faisal Islamic Bank, Niger; Islamic Investment Company, Niger; Islamic Investment Company, Sudan, Export Development Bank, Sudan; Dar al Mal al Islamic, Geneva; Islamic Investment Service Company, Geneva; Faisal Islamic Bank, Senegal; Islamic Investment Company, Senegal; Al Baraka Bank–Sudan, Saudi Sudanese Bank, Sudan, Al Baraka Turkish Finance House, Turkey
1985	7	Banque Al Wava Mauritanienne Islamique, Mauritana; Faisal Finance Institution, Turkey Al Baraka Turkish Finance House, ABC Islamic Bank, Bahrain, B.R.R. Intl. Modaraba, Pakistan, First Habib Modaraba, Pakistan, Al Shamal Islamic Bank, Sudan
1987	7	Al Amin Bank, Bahrain, LTV Capital Modaraba, Pakistan, Modaraba Al- Mali, Pakistan, Standard Chartered Modaraba, Pakistan, Al Rajhi Bank, Saudi Arabia, Worker' National Bank, Sudan, Lariba American Finance House, USA
1988	4	Egyptian Saudi Finance Bank, Egypt National Islamic Bank, Jordan Islamic Bank, South Africa, Kuwait Turkish Evkaf Finance House, Turkey

Contd...

1989	5	Muslim Community Cooperative, Australia, B.F. Modaraba, Pakistan, First National Modaraba, Pakistan, First Prudential Modaraba, Pakistan, Al Baraka Bank Ltd, South Africa
1990	2	Arab Islamic Bank, Bahrain, International Islamic Bank, Qatar
1991	13	Banque Al-Baraka D'Algerie, Algeria, Export Development Bank of Iran, Al Baraka Bank Lebanon, First Elite Modaraba Pakistan, ,First Fidelity Leasing Modaraba, Pakistan, First General Leasing Modaraba, Pakistan, First Habib Bank, Pakistan, Modaraba, First Pak Modaraba, First UDL Modaraba, Pakistan ,Guardian Modaraba, Pakistan, Modaraba al Tijarah, Pakistan, Trust Modaraba, Pakistan ,Anadolu Finans Kurumu A.S. Turkey,
1992	7	Animal Resources Bank, Sudan, Al Tawfeek Co. for Investment Funds, Saudi Arabia, First Equity Modaraba, Pakistan, The International Investor, Kuwait, PT. Bank Syariah Mualmalat, Indonesia, Kauthar Bank, Azerbaizan, United Bank of Albania
1993	3	First Allied Bank Modaraba, Pakistan, First Punjab Modaraba, Pakistan, Omdurman National Bank, Sudan
1994	5	Unity Modaraba, Pakistan, First Imrooz Modaraba, Pakistan, Faysal Bank Limited, Pakistan, Investment Dar, Kuwait, Arab Gambian Islamic Bank Limited, Gambia
1995	7	Social Investment Bank Ltd, Bangladesh, First Paramount Modaraba, Pakistan, Palestine Islamic Bank, Gedarif Investment Bank, Sudan, Savings & Social Development Bank, Sudan, Islamic Bank of Yemen for Finance & Investment, Yemen, Tadhamon Intl Islamic Bank, Yemen
1996	2	Oasis Group Holdings (PTY) Ltd, Oasis, South Africa, Asya Finans Kurumu A.S., Turkey

Contd...

1997	5	Saba Islamic Bank, Yemen, Abu Dhabi Islamic Bank, UAE, Financial Investment Bank, Pakistan, First Investment, Kuwait, Investors Bank, Bahrain
1998	5	Islamic Intl Arab Bank plc, Jordan, Al Madar Finance & Investment, Kuwait, Gulf Investment House, Kuwait, Badr-Forte Bank, Russia, HSBC Amanah, UAE
1999	8	Farmers' Commercial Bank, Sudan, First Finance, Qatar, Bank Muamalat, Malaysia, The Intl Leasing & Investment Co., Kuwait, Osoul Leasing & Finance, Kuwait, Saman Bank, Iran, PT Bank Syariah Mandiri, Indonesia, Gulf Finance House (BSC) E.C., Bahrain,
2000	5	Shamil Bank of Bahrain B.S.C., Bahrain, Shahjalal Islami Bank Limited, Bangladesh, Bosnia Bank International, Bosnia Herzegovina, Islamic Development Bank of Brunei Bhd, Brunei, Amlak Finance PJSC, UAE
2001	3	Eqtesad Novid, Iran, Persian Bank, Iran, Fayzan Manufacturing Modaraba, Pakistan,
2002	5	Kuwait Finance House (Bahrain) B.S.C., Bahrain, First Standard Investment Bank Ltd, Pakistan, The Islamic Bank of Thailand, Sharjah Islamic Bank, UAE, Shamil Bank of Yemen & Bahrain, Yemen
2003	1	The Securities House, Kuwait,
2004	2	Emirates Islamic Bank, UAE, Islamic Bank of Britain Plc,UK
2005	2	RHB Islamic Bank, Malaysia, Kurdistan Intl' Bank for Investment & Development, Iraq
2006	1	European Islamic Investment Bank Plc,UK
Total	154	

Source: Islamic Finance Directory, General Counsel for Islamic Banks and Financial Institutions, Bahrain.

4.3 Evaluation of Islamic Financial Institutions

The comprehensive databank developed and managed by the Council for Islamic Banks and Financial Institutions for the purpose of evaluation has classified IFIs into three groups according to the following two elements: (a) current accounts, and (b) investment accounts.

Group A comprises of IFIs having current accounts and may have other type of deposits. This group necessarily comprises of commercial or comprehensive banks regardless of their classification by the regulatory authorities of the system they work in.

Group B comprises of IFIs having saving and/or investment deposits. This group necessarily comprises of investment banks and financial institutions regardless of their classification by the regulatory authorities of the systems they work in.

Group C comprises of IFIs that neither have current accounts nor accept deposits. According to the international conventions, this group of IFIs is considered as "financial institutions". They have not been addressed in detail in this study as they are very rare and small in size.

This study is dominated by Group A that had around 96.3 percent of global IFIs assets in the year 2003 while Group 2 had only 3.7 percent. This study is restricted to the achievements of banks and investment institutions that are fully *Shari'ah* compliant. Therefore, it does not cover Islamic windows of conventional institutions, Islamic insurance institutions and Islamic investment funds. The information in this section of the study covers 157 IFIs all over the world during the period 1993-2000.

4.3.1. IFIs Total Assets: IFIs assets have witnessed high growth since 1993. It has grown at an average annual growth rate of 22.94 percent to reach US$ 174.3 billion in the year 2003 from US$ 53.3 billion in 1993. The highest annual growth rate of the IFIs (during 1994-2003) was in the year 2004 when the total assets increased to US$ 154.6 billion from US$ 53.8 billion in the previous year. The lowest annual growth rate was in the year 2002 when IFIs total assets decreased to around US$ 145 billion from US$ 269 billion in the year 2001 with a negative growth rate of 46.12 percent. That decrease was due to the devaluation of the Iranian currency against the US$ (with an exchange rate of 7922 Riyals for each Dollar) in March 2002 while it was 1750 Riyal vs Dollar in the year 2001. This effect is clearly explained when taking into consideration the geographical distribution of IFIs of which Iranian banks formed 80 percent of the total assets in the year 2001.

In 2003, IFIs assets continued growing with an annual growth rate of 20.48 percent. When comparing IFIs assets' growth rates to the Arab commercial banks during the period 1998-2003, this study found that the growth rate of IFIs were much higher than their counterparts in the Arab commercial banks. With exception of the decrease of IFIs assets in 2002, the lowest annual growth rate of IFIs was 15.25 percent in 2002. IFIs also recorded 23.58 percent, 39.65 percent, and 20.48 percent in the years 1999, 2000 and 2003 respectively. On the other side, Arab commercial banks' annual growth rate was 7.74 percent in 2003, and did not exceed 8.2 percent in the period considered for review.

This distinction of IFIs assets' growth rates is due to smaller sizes of the bases of calculating the rates than their counterparts of the Arab commercial banks. This is in addition to the fact that IFIs is an emergent industry in comparison to the Arab banking industry. If IFIs growth rate continues with the same pattern of around 20 percent, Council for Islamic Banks and Financial Institutions (CIBAFI) projection shows that IFIs total assets will be US$ 1081.7 billion in 2013. When considering a modest growth pattern ranging between 10 to 15 percent, IFIs total assets would be in the range of US$ 453 billion to around US$ 700 $ billion by the year 2013.

4.3.2 IFIs Total Assets: Country wise: Although IFIs are distributed all over the world, its assets' largest geographical intensity in 2003 was in the Middle East (including Egypt, Iran, Jordan, Lebanon, Palestine, Turkey and Yemen) with a proportion of 62 percent; then comes the GCC (including Bahrain, KSA, Kuwait, Qatar and UAE) with a 29 percent share, the rest of Asia at 7 percent, Africa at 2 percent, and

Europe and America with less than 1 percent. Iran is on the top of the list of countries incubating the largest IFIs in terms of assets, followed by Saudi Arabia, Kuwait, UAE, Malaysia and Bahrain. IFIs assets in each of the rest of countries did not exceed US$ 1 billion in 2003.

In terms of assets' average annual growth rates during 1999-2003, five countries had growth rates which equalled or exceeded 50 percent. Brunei had the highest average growth rate of 474.18 percent, followed by Malaysia at 102.88 percent, Yemen at 82.80 percent and Indonesia at 72.5 percent.

A. Iran: Islamic Banking in Iran was shaped by the overall reorganization of the economy after the 1979 Revolution. The structure of the Islamic banking system was put in place in 1983 by issuing the Interest-Free Banking Law of 1983. This law was implemented in March 1984, and banks were given 18 months to complete transformation to Islamic banking principles.

In spite of the high devaluation of its local currency against the US Dollar, Iran stayed on the top of countries incubating IFIs with the largest asset size. Iranian IFIs' had a proportion of 57.81 percent of IFIs' total assets with US$ 101 billion in 2003, in comparison to US$ 80.2 billion in 2002 and US$ 215 billion in 2001.

When taking into consideration the size of Iranian IFIs' assets in the local currency, this study observed a real continuous growth with an average rate of 38 percent and size of Riyal 852 trillion; Iranian assets were experiencing a high growth rate of 75 percent in 2002 when the local currency devalued by 61 percent.

B. Saudi Arabia: Being in the second rank at the global level and the first at the GCC level, Saudi IFIs' total assets was US$ 20.4 billion in 2003. Saudi IFIs' grew at an average annual growth rate of 13 percent during 1999-2003. Al Rajhi Company for Banking and Investment was the largest player there with an average annual growth rate of 11.2 percent during the respective period. In 1999, Saudi IFIs witnessed the coming of Al Jazeera Bank as a new player that increased its assets from US$ 1.4 billion in 2000 to US$ 2.4 billion in 2003, witnessing an average growth rate of 34.5 percent. Regarding the Saudi Arabian statistics in this study, it has to be pointed out that it did not take into consideration National Commercial Bank (NCB) that was established in 1953, and went to the Islamic banking in 1990. NCB's total assets were US$ 130.414 billion in 2004 with 161 branches offering Islamic banking out of 248 total branches. NCB has converted itself into full fledged Islamic bank since 2004.

C. Kuwait: Kuwaiti IFIs' assets amounted to US$ 13.7 billion in 2003, a matter that enabled Kuwait to be in the third rank at the global level, and second rank at the GCC level. Kuwait recorded an average annual growth rate of 18 percent during 1999-2003 while this rate was averaged at 34 percent during 2001-2003. The largest Kuwait player—Kuwait Finance House—achieved an average annual growth rate of 25.7 percent during 2001-2003, while A'Ayan Company for Leasing and Investment achieved a 130.4 percent growth, International Investor, 62.5 percent, Aref Investment Group, 60.5 percent, Investment Dar, 58 percent, The International Leasing and Investment Company 42.4 percent, First Investment, 40 percent, Osol Company for Leasing and Finance, 31.3 percent, and Gulf Investment House, 30.5 percent. The new players' average annual growth rates ranged from 5 percent to 29 percent.

D. UAE: UAE was in the fourth rank at the global level with assets amounting to US$ 9.4 billion in 2003 and average annual growth rate of 30.5 percent during 1999-2003. The large size of Dubai Islamic Bank at US$ 6.2 billion, the average annual growth rate of Abu Dhabi Islamic Bank at 46.5 percent, and entrance of the new comer–Sharjah Islamic Bank, in 2000, were the main reasons for UAE to achieve the highest average growth rate in the GCC during 1999-2003.

E. Malaysia: With total assets amounting to US$ 5.5 billion, Malaysia was globally in the fifth rank. Malaysian

IFIs' assets average annual growth rate was 103 percent during 1999-2003 and is the highest one all over the world after Brunei. This is due to the growth of Bank Islam Malaysia and Bank Muamalat Malaysia. Bank Muamalat Malaysia was established in 1999 with total assets of US$ 923 billion that doubled in 2003 to reach US$ 1.929 billion. Established early in 1983, Bank Islam Malaysia witnessed an accelerated growth rates that increased its assets to US$ 3.617 billion in 2003 from US$ 468 million in 1999.

F. Bahrain: Bahrain IFIs' assets increased to US$ 4.1 billion in 2003 with an annual growth rate of 30.43 percent which was the highest in the GCC in that year. However, Bahraini IFIs' assets grew at an average annual growth rate of 11.65 percent during 1999-2003. Arcapita and Gulf Finance were the main institutions which contributed to the average annual growth rate in Bahrain during 1999-2003. While Arcapita recorded a 48.8 percent average annual growth rate and was locally ranked no. 2 in terms of assets in 2003, GFH recorded a 43.7 percent growth during the period under review and was locally ranked no. 6 in 2003. Bahraini IFIs was supported by the entrance of the Kuwait Finance House/Bahrain which was locally ranked no. 6 with assets amounting to US$ 268 million in 2003 after it had grown at a rate of 185 percent from US$ 94 million in 2002. Shamil Bank of Bahrain–the largest bank in Bahrain, had assets amounting to US$ 12 billion in 2003 after an average annual growth rate of 1.4 percent during 1999-2003. Bahrain Islamic Bank–the third local bank in terms of assets, achieved an average annual growth rate of 8.6 percent during 1999-2003 while the fourth local bank in terms of assets–Al Baraka Islamic Bank, had an average annual growth rate of 15.8 percent.

G. Sudan: The concept of Islamic banking was introduced first in the Sudan in August 1977 by establishing Faisal Bank (Sudan). Other Islamic banks followed. *Shari'ah* laws were launched in September 1983. Following this enactment, banks were asked to change their business activities to be consistent with *Shari'ah* rules. A year later, in September 1984, the whole banking system was transformed by presidential decree to work on Islamic basis. However, due to changes in governments during 1985-89, the process of Islamizing banking system was interrupted many times. Since 1990, the Central Bank has seriously adopted the principle of Islamic banking. Borrowing and lending transactions have since been carried out on Islamic norms of financing. Various purchases and sales agreements are conducted on the basis of profit-sharing arrangements that determine *ex-post* the rate of return.

Following this transformation, and since mid-1991, the Central Bank used to apply monetary and credit policies based on Islamic banking requirements. Effective rates of return on bank lending are estimated and are not pre-fixed like the interest rate. On the liability side, banks are required to replace time deposits by investment deposits so that returns to depositors are according to the *pro rata* principles of profit-sharing. Heavy administrative and financial penalties upon circumventing Islamic banking principles by banks have been incorporated into the *Financial Institutions and Banks Act, (1991)*, introduced into effect as early as 1992. In 2003, Sudanese IFIs' assets increased to US$ 2.9 billion with an average annual growth rate of 31 percent during 1999-2003. Umdurman National Bank was the largest Sudanese bank with assets amounting to US$ 725 million in 2003, followed by Al Khartoum Bank at US$ 303 million followed by a group of 9 banks with assets ranging between US$ 100-170 million, Saudi French Bank at US$ 169 million, Saudi Sudanese Bank at US$ 160 million, Al Nilein Bank Group at US$ 153 million, Workers Bank at US$ 134 million, Animal Resources Bank at US$ 134 million, Tadamon Islamic Bank at US$ 114 million, and Islamic Co-operative Bank for Development at US$ 109 million.

H. Egypt: In 2003, Egypt witnessed a decrease in the growth of the IFIs assets due to the special conditions of the International Islamic Bank for Investment and Development whose information of 2003 could not be accessed, although the total assets of the Bank was US$ 838.2 million in 2002. Assets of Egyptian IFIs had an unstable and low growth rates during the period 1999-2003, a fact that placed Egypt a step backward in the international ranking of IFIs assets in 2003 (the eighth rank). Faisal Islamic Bank was considered as one of the pioneers as it was established in 1977. Since then, Faisal Islamic Bank had increased its assets to reach US$ 2.264 billion in 2003 when Egyptian Saudi Finance Bank got an assets of US$ 548 million.

I. Qatar: Asset size of Qatari IFIs increased to amount to US$ 2.8 billion in 2003 with an annual growth rate of 22.43 percent from the previous year. However, Qatari IFIs got an average annual growth rate of 13.48 percent during the period 1999-2003. With total assets exceeding US$ 1.5 billion in 2003, Qatar Islamic Bank was considered as the largest player although it achieved an average annual growth rate of 8.2 percent during 1999-2003. While Qatar International Islamic Bank got an average annual growth rate of 19.4 percent for total assets of US$ 1.1 billion in 2003, First Finance had recorded a high annual growth rate since 2001 with an average of 160 percent for total assets that reached US$ 183.3 million in 2003.

J. Turkey: Turkey is considered as one of the pioneer countries incubating the Islamic banking and finance. The first IFI in Turkey appeared in 1983 under the title of Special Finance House and under the Turkish Decree for that year. CIBAFI statistics for the year 2003 covers the largest 3 finance houses, viz. Al Turkish Kuwaiti Awqaf Finance House, Al Baraka Turkish Finance House, and Famili Komro Finance House. Their assets in 2003 were US$ 805, 843, and 511 million respectively. Thus, the total assets of Turkish IFIs exceeded US$ 2.159 billion in 2003, a matter that made Turkey ranked at no. 10 at the global level in terms of countries incubating IFIs' assets.

K. Brunei: With a total asset base of US$ 2.060 billion,

Brunei was at the 11th rank in 2003. In addition, this country recorded the highest average annual growth rate of IFIs assets of 474 percent during the period 1999-2003. This large growth was due to the establishment of Brunei Islamic Development Bank in 1999 with total assets of US$ 1.309 billion in 2003 and Brunei Islamic Bank in 2000 with US$ 751 million in assets in 2003. Before the establishment of these two banks, there had been only a small Islamic financial institution with a total assets of US$ 45 million in 2001 compared to US$ 20 million in the previous year.

L. Jordan: Assets of IFI's in Jordan increased to reach US$ 1.965 billion in 2003 with an average annual growth rate of 11.19 percent during the period 1999-2003. Being among the pioneer IFIs all over the world, Jordan Islamic Bank owned around 70 percent of the IFIs total assets in Jordan in 2003. The Bank was established early in 1978, and since then it has been distinctive of stable and continuous growth. Two other IFIs are working in Jordan namely, Beit Al Mal for saving (established in 1983) and Investment Arab Islamic International Bank that have been witnessing a fast growth rates since their establishment in 1988, to own around 28 percent of IFIs' total assets in Jordan.

M. Bangladesh: With total assets amounting to US$ 1.816 billion in 2003, Bangladesh was ranked 13th at the global level. Islami Bank Bangladesh (established in 1983, owned around 75 percent of the IFIs assets in Bangladesh in 2003), Public Investment Bank (established in 1995, owned around 19 percent of the IFIs assets in Bangladesh in 2003), Shah Jalal Bank (established in 2001, owned around 6 percent of the IFIs assets in Bangladesh in 2003). There were also 3 additional Islamic banking subsidiaries working in Bangladesh, viz. Al Mashriq Bank which started its activities in 1987 under the name "Al Baraka Bangladesh Bank", Al Arafa Islamic Bank which was established in 1995, and the branch of Shamil Bank of Bahrain which started its activities in 1997. This is in addition to the Islamic Finance and Investment Company which was established in 2001 as a non-banking Islamic financial institution.

N. Pakistan: Leaders of Pakistani financial sector have tried to comply with Islamic rules for more than 16 years. However, the country is still conducting the required researches and studies required to find solutions for several pending questions. State Bank of Pakistan has recently issued new regulations allowing banks to apply for a dual banking system (Islamic and conventional) either through establishing independent or subsidiary Islamic banks. With this respect, six licenses of establishing Islamic branches have been granted to six conventional banks during the last few years. On the other side, there are three full-fledged *Shari'ah* compliant Pakistani banks: Al Meezan Commercial Islamic Bank, Faisal Bank, and Al Baraka Islamic Investment Bank. This is in addition to 34 Mudaraba companies, licensed to work according to *Shari'ah* rules, with total assets to US$ 348 million in the year 2003. The total assets of all Pakistani IFIs amounted to US$ 1.058 million, a fact that made Pakistan in the 14th rank at the global level.

O. Indonesia: Due to the issuance of the Islamic Banking Act in 1998, Indonesia has witnessed a distinctive growth in IFIs' assets since the last few years. Indonesian IFIs' assets have grown from US$ 59.8 million in 1998 to reach US$ 795 million in 2003. Indonesia is one of the countries having high average annual growth rate of assets at 72.5 percent during the period 1999-2003 preceded by Brunei, Malaysia, and Yemen. In 1992, Bank Muamalt Indonesia started its activities and stayed alone in the marketplace as an Islamic bank till 1999 when a conventional bank converted to Islamic banking under the name Sharia' Manderi. This Bank achieved high average annual growth rate of 77 percent during 1999-2003, an issue that made its balance sheet contain more than 50 percent of the Indonesian IFIs' assets. Moreover, there are more than 85 small-sized Islamic financial institutions classified as rural development banks.

P. Yemen: Although establishment of Islamic banks started lately in Yemen, the average annual growth rate of assets was 82.80 percent during the period 1999-2003. After the issuance of Islamic Banking Act in 1996, three Islamic banks were established: Yemeni Islamic Bank for Finance and Investment, Tadamon Islamic Bank, and Saba Islamic Bank. They were followed by Yemen Bahrain Shamil Bank which was established in 2002. Yemeni IFIs' assets doubled from US$ 342 million to US$ 726 million during the period 2001-2003. However, Tadamon Islamic Bank had around 60 percent of Yemeni IFIs assets in 2003.

4.3.3 IFIs Assets: Institution-wise: Commercial and/or comprehensive banks (coming under Group A of our classification) had an average annual growth rate that was approximately the same as IFIs assets' average annual growth rate during the period 1998-2003 (10.57 percent for IFIs total assets and 10.68 percent for Group A). This is obvious because Group A IFIs had around 96.3 percent of the global IFIs' assets. Group B's average annual growth rate of assets was 24.51 percent as a result of the low base of assets used in calculating the growth rates.

Group A (Commercial and/or Investment Banks): At the global level, eight Iranian banks were among the top twenty asset wise commercial banks in 2003. Bank Mille Iran at US$ 27.57 billion, Bank Sadat Iran at US$ 18.37 billion and Bank Mellat at US$ 17.95 billion were in the first three ranks respectively. However, the 5th, 7th, 9th, 10th and 14th ranks were for Bank Tejarat at US$ 10.37 billion, Bank Sepah at US$ 9.84 billion, Bank Keshavarzi at US$ 5.57 billion, Bank of Maskan at US$ US$ billion, and Bank Refah at US$ 2.3 billion respectively. GCC commercial banks reserved 6 ranks among the top twenty. Al Rajhi Banking and Investment Corp. was in the 4th rank with total assets of US$ 17.25 billion, Kuwait Finance House with US$ 10.31 billion was in the 6th rank, Dubai Islamic Bank with US$ 6.2 billion in the 8th, Abu Dhabi Islamic Bank with US$ 2.51 billion in the 12th rank, Al

Jazeera Bank with US$ 2.4 billion in the 13th, and Qatar Islamic Bank with US$ 1.54 billion at no. 17. The two Malaysian banks, Bank Islam Malaysia with US$ 3.62 billion and Bank Muamalat Malaysia with US$ 1.93 billion were in the 11th and 16th ranks respectively.

The 15th, 18th, 19th, and 20th ranks were for Faisal Islamic Bank/Egypt at US$ 2.26 billion, Jordan Islamic Bank at US$ 1.37 billion, Islami Bank Bangladesh at US$ 1.36 billion, and Brunei Islamic Bank at US$ 1.31 billion respectively. It can be inferred from the list of top twenty IFIs growth rates during the period 1999-2003, that the top twenty commercial banks got total assets of 85 percent of the total IFIs' assets in 2003. After growing at an average annual growth rate of 9.94 percent during 1998-2003, the total assets of the top twenty amounted to US$ 149.04 billion in 2003. Bank Islam Malaysia recorded an extra ordinary average annual growth rate of 93.12 percent during 1998-2003 when its total assets grew from US$ 0.34 billion in 1998 to US$ 3.62 billion in 2003. The greatest jump of the Bank was in 2000 when its assets grew at a rate of 374.47 percent and increased from US$ 0.47 billion in the previous year to US$ 2.23 billion in 2000.

However, there were 5 banks among the top twenty with an average annual growth rate which was more than the growth rate of all IFIs put together. Abu Dhabi Islamic Bank (with 46.49 percent average annual growth) was on top of these banks, followed by Al Jazeera Bank at 34.52 percent, Islami Bank Bangladesh at 23.20 percent, and Bank Muamalat Malaysia at 21.40 percent. Al Rajhi Banking and Investment Corporation and Kuwait Finance House that led the list of asset size, got an average annual growth rate of 11.23 percent and 13.40 percent respectively.

Group B (Investment Banks and Financial Institutions): The total number of investment bank and financial institutions was 53 in 2003. Their total assets were around US$ 6.5 billion in that year. The total assets of the top 15 of this Group amounted to US$ 5.6 billion in 2003 with a proportion of 88 percent of the total assets of all investment banks and financial institutions (Group B). The entire top 15 were GCC institutions, of which there were 9 Kuwaiti, 4 Bahraini, 1 Saudi and 1 Kuwaiti.

A. Investment Dar Company: With total assets amounted to US$ 941 million, Investment Dar Company was the largest member of Group B. Its assets grew at an average annual growth rate of 27.97 percent during 1999-2003. Being established in 1994, it is considered as one of the first Islamic investment Kuwaiti companies.

B. Arcapita Bank: In terms of assets, the second rank of Group B was Arcapita Bank. Being distinctive by high annual growth rates, the Arcapita's average annual growth rate was 48.78 percent during 1999-2003. Arcapita is considered as number one investment bank in Bahrain.

C. Al Tawfeek Company for Investment Funds: In spite of the decrease of assets in 2001, Al Tawfeek was able to be in the third rank after it grew at 23.5 percent and 3.6 percent in 2002 and 2003 respectively.

D. Aa'yan Company for Leasing and Investment: Although it was established lately in 1999, Aa'yan was able to increase its assets from US$ 73.5 million in the establishment year to US$ 651 million in 2003, a fact that enabled Aa'yan to be in the fourth rank.

E. Securities House: The Company started as conventional institution in 1982. However, its general assembly took the decision to convert it into Islamic banking and finance in the year 2003. The total assets in the conversion year were US$ 335 million.

F. Aref Investment Group: The Company was established in 1975 under the name "Arab European Company for Financial Management". In 1998, its general assembly took the decision to convert into Islamic banking and finance. Aref Investment Group witnessed a high growth rate in 2002 of 76 percent.

G. Osoul Company for Leasing and Finance: Osoul was established in 1999. With total assets of US$ 279 million, Osoul was in the 7th rank in 2003.

H. Gulf Finance House: As an Islamic investment bank, GFH was established in Bahrain in 1999. GHF was able to increase its assets to reach US$ 25 million in 2003 with an average annual growth rate of 44 percent during 1999-2003.

I. The International Investor: Having been established in Kuwait since 1992, TII is one of the oldest Islamic investment companies.

With total assets amounting to US$ 247 million, TII was ranked 9th in 2003 with an exceptional increase of its annual growth rate in 2001 when its assets increased from US$ 82 million to US$ 241 million.

J. Arab Banking Corporation/Islamic: ABC started offering Islamic banking through its Islamic Bank in 1985. The ABC Islamic subsidiary was in the 10th rank among the members of Group B. ABC's total assets were US$ 245 million in 2003 with an average annual growth rate of 10 percent during 1998-2003.

K. Gulf Investment House: With total assets of US$ 108 million, Gulf Investment House started working in Kuwait in 1998. GIH total assets were US$ 208 million in 2003, with an average annual growth rate of 18 percent during the period 1998-2003.

L. First Finance: First Finance was established in Qatar in 1999. During 1999-2003, First Finance was distinctive of its average annual growth rate of 160.11 percent by which it increased its total assets from US$ 15 million to more than US$ 182 million in 2003.

M. Al Amin Bank: Al Amin Bank is part of Al Baraka Banking Group. It was established in Bahrain in 1987 under the name "Al Amin Company for Securities and Investment Funds". In May 2001, Al Amin was converted to an investment Islamic bank. With total assets of US$ 175 million, Al Amin Bank was in the 13th rank among Islamic investment banks and financial institutions at the global level.

N. First Investments: First Investment was able to achieve accelerated growth rates during 2001-2003. The highest growth rate in 2003 at 68 percent in total assets from the previous year was due to the increase in the paid up capital and the profits of that year.

O. International Leasing Company: Since its incorporation in 1999, the International Leasing Company had been achieving reputable growth although there were no increases in the paid up capital. Its total assets grew at 14.6 percent, 41 percent and 30 percent in the years 2001, 2002, 2003 respectively.

4.3.4 Total Deposits in IFIs: After growing at an average annual growth rate of 14.08 percent during 1999-2003, total IFIs deposits amounted to US$ 137.58 billion in 2003 with an increase of US$ 43.05 billion above that amount in 1998. It is very important to mention that the above-mentioned average annual growth rate of 14.08 percent does not reflect the actual growth rate of IFIs deposits. This is due to the fact that the calculation of this rate includes Iranian IFIs total deposits in US$. If this effect is set aside, the average annual growth rate of IFIs total deposits (except Iran) will be 18.15 percent during the period 1999-2003.

As IFIs total assets are found intensively in the Middle East and the GCC region, IFIs total deposits are consequently found intensively in those regions. IFIs Middle East total deposits formed 62.16 percent of IFIs total deposits in 2003, whereas IFIs GCC total deposits formed 28.65 percent of IFIs total deposits. At the country level, Iranian IFIs' total deposits was the greatest with amounting to US$ 78.26 billion followed by Saudi Arabia at US$ 16.25 billion, Kuwait at US$ 9.57 billion, and then UAE at US$ 8.1 billion.

A. Deposits of Group A (Commercial/Comprehensive Islamic Banks and Financial Institutions): Within Group A, the total deposits of 25 banks and financial institution amounted to US$ 123.565 billion forming around 90 percent of IFIs total deposits in 2003. Out of these 25 institutions, there were 9 Iranian banks. The other 16 were headed by the largest three players: Al Rajihi/Saudi Arabia at US$ 13.307 billion, Kuwait Finance House/Kuwait at US$ 8.02 billion and Dubai Islamic Bank/UAE at US$ 5.5 billion.

This was followed by Bank Islam Malaysia/Malaysia which was able to increase its deposit portfolio from US$ 257 million in 1998 to US$ 3.289 billion in 2003, Faisal Islamic Bank/Egypt at US$ 2.126 billion, Al Jazeera Bank/Saudi Arabia at US$ 2.151 billion, and the Abu Dhabi Islamic Bank/UAE at US$ 2.01 billion.

B. Deposits of Group B (Investment Banks and Financial Institutions): Although this Group has only investment deposits, three of its members had deposits exceeding US$ 500 million in 2003, viz. Al Tawfeek Company for Investment Funds at US$ 794.088 million, Investment Dar at US$ 623.577 million, and Arcapita Bank at US$ 595.234 million.

These institutions were followed by three institutions with deposits between US$ 200-500 million: A'ayan Company for Leasing and Investment at US$ 438 million, Arab Banking Corporation/Islamic at US$ 392 million and Osoul Company for Leasing and Finance at US$ 216 million.

4.3.5 Growth of Current Accounts: Current accounts formed an average of 37 percent of IFIs total deposits during 1998-2003. The peak of IFIs current accounts was in 2001 when it amounted to US$ 100.96 billion and grew at an annual growth rate of 46.23 percent. In 2003, current accounts formed around 41 percent of IFIs' total deposits.

There were 12 banks with this ratio exceeding 85 percent. Al Rajihi/Saudi Arabia and Workers National Bank/Sudan had this ratio close to 100 percent. At the country level, this ratio exceeded 60 percent in 8 countries—Lebanon at 89 percent, Niger at 83 percent, Gambia at 74 percent, Algeria at 71 percent, Sudan at 66 percent, Russia at 65 percent, Bosnia at 62 percent, and Saudi Arabia at 60 percent.

4.3.6 IFIs Shareholders' Equity: IFIs total equity decreased from US$ 16.94 billion in 2001 to US$ 13.38 billion in 2002 due to the devaluation of the Iranian currency. However, IFIs total equity amounted to US$ 14.97 billion in 2003 with an annual growth rate of 12 percent from the previous year. Although IFIs assets in the GCC formed around 29 percent of total IFIs assets in 2003, total equity of IFIs in that region was the largest in that year when it amounted to US$ 7.3 billion and formed around 49 percent of IFIs total equity. In light of the economic boom in the GCC region, that fact may be considered as an indicator of the success of the GCC IFIs in maximising the equity of their shareholders especially when comparing the assets of their counterparts in the Middle East and Iran. IFIs are distinctive by the small size of their paid up capital.

According to CIBAFI statistics for the year 2003, there were around 59 percent of IFIs with paid up capital of less than US$ 25 million, while there were around 23 percent of IFIs with paid up capital between US$ 26 million and US$ 100 million, 12 percent of IFIs with paid up capital between US$ 101 million and US$ 200 million, 4 percent of IFIs with paid up capital between US$ 201 million and US$ 300 million, and 2 percent of IFIs with paid up capital exceeding US$ 301 million including one institution (Al Rajihi Corporation for Banking and Investment) with paid up capital close to US$ 600 million.

4.3.7 IFIs Shareholders' Equity: Country-wise: At the country level, Iran led the list of IFIs equity-wise top 15 countries. Iran formed around 36 percent of IFIs total shareholders' equity with US$ 5.42 billion in 2003. However, when comparing Iranian IFIs' equity to their assets, we found that equity to assets ratio did not exceed 5 percent in 2003. That fact reflected the large size of the external resources and liabilities of the Iranian IFIs, in light of a banking system that works only according to *Shari'ah* rules. Due to the large size of shareholders equity of Al Rajihi Corporation, Saudi Arabia was in the second rank followed by Kuwait, Bahrain, and UAE. It is important here to point out that the four GCC countries with Iran formed around 83 percent of IFIs total equity in 2003. Moreover, the list of top 15 countries formed around 98.6 percent of IFIs total equity. This fact emphasizes the small size of the capital base of the Islamic financial institutions all over the world and affects the nature of their activities that mainly focus on retail banking.

4.3.8 IFIs Shareholders' Equity: Institution-wise:

A. Group A (Commercial/Comprehensive Banks and Financial Institutions): With a total shareholders' equity closed to US$ 2 billion, Al Rajihi Corporation for Banking and Investments was on the first rank at the global level. This was after its shareholders' equity had grown at an annual growth rate of 6 percent from 2002 to 2003. The second rank was for Bank Milli Iran and Bank Saderat Iran with total shareholders' equity amounting to US$ 1.5 billion and US$ 1.1 billion respectively.

After growing at an average annual growth rate of 11.12 percent during 2002-2003, Kuwait Finance House got the fourth rank with total shareholders' equity amounting to US$ 965.03 million. Bank Millat Iran was in the fifth rank with total shareholders' equity amounting to US$ 513.88 million, while Dubai Islamic Bank was in the sixth rank after maximizing its shareholders' equity by 27.31 percent in 2002. The list of top 20 equity-wise commercial/comprehensive Islamic banks and financial institutions formed around 69 percent of IFIs total shareholders' equity in 2003 when its total shareholders' equity amounted to US$ 10.37 billion with a growth rate of 9.59 percent from the previous year.

B. Group B: Investment Banks and Financial Companies: The total equity of Group B (Investment Banks and Financial Institutions) amounted to US$ 2.57 billion in 2003 and formed around 17 percent of IFIs total shareholders' equity. The top 15 equity-wise of Group B had shareholders' equity amounting to US$ 2.23 billion and formed around 15 percent of total IFIs shareholders equity. At the global level, Al Tawfeek Company for Investment Funds was at the first rank with total shareholders' equity amounting to US$ 415.63 million in 2003 with an annual growth rate of 14 percent from the previous year.

The second rank was for Investment Dar—one of 11 Kuwaiti institutions included in the top 15 list, with total shareholders' equity amounting to US$ 228.73 million after growing at an annual growth rate of 82 percent in 2003. The third and fourth ranks were for The International Investor and Arcapita Investment Bank with shareholders' equity amounting to US$ 218.45 million and US$ 205.73 million respectively.

The highest average annual growth rate of shareholders equity in Group B during 2002-2003 was for First Investment at 59.25 percent, a matter that put the company in the 10th rank after increasing its shareholders' equity from US$ 47.17 million in 2001 to US$ 112.69 million in 2003.

4.3.9 IFIs Net Profit and Reserves: After growing at an average annual growth rate of 14.3 percent and 21.88 percent during 1995-2003, IFIs total reserves and net profits amounted respectively to US$ 3.88 billion and US$ 2.74 billion in 2003. All the decrease of the IFIs accounts was mainly due to the devaluation of the Iranian currency in 2002, the decrease of those accounts in 1998 was due to the fact that the former International Association for Islamic Banks had considered all banks working in Pakistan as Islamic depending on the Pakistani governmental resolution at that time to gradually adopt the Islamic banking system.

However, the successive Pakistani governments decided to adopt a dual banking system (conventional and Islamic). CIBAFI statistics showed that there were 48 institutions with growth rates of net profit above the IFIs 51 percent in 2003. Among the mentioned institutions, there were 5 with annual growth rate above 500 percent, while there were 11 institutions with annual growth rate of net profits between 200 percent-499 percent, and 18 institutions between 18 percent-99 percent in that year.

4.3.10. IFIs Total Investments (1998-2003): The average ratio of IFIs total investments to IFIs total assets was 64.64 percent during 1998-2003; while IFIs total investment was growing at an average annual growth rate of 17 percent during the same period to reach US$ 134.26 billion in 2003. While the average ratio of total investments to total assets was 62.88 percent during the period 1998-2003 in commercial banks, it was 88.23 percent in investment banks. This can be explained by the fact that commercial banks usually have larger proportion of liquid assets to meet the requirements of the current accounts, while investment banks do not. This explanation is also supported by the difference between the ratios of cash and equivalents to total assets in the two groups (11.62 percent as an average of the ratio for commercial during 1998-2003 and 4.55 percent for investment banks during the same period).

4.3.11 IFIs Return on Equity ROE (2001-2003): Return on Equity (ROE) is considered as one of the most important profitability indicators that should be benchmarked for investment and commercial banks. As the historical data of the IFIs shareholders' equity is not available, we are not able to produce a historical benchmark because this indicator is very time sensitive and should be studied for periods exceeding 10 years. For IFIs, the average annual ROE during 2001-2003 was 15.39 percent which is much close to its counterpart, the American banks at 15.6 percent. The highest ROE for the IFIs was in 2003 at 18.27 percent. At the institutional level, there were 22 commercial banks and financial institutions with an average ROE above 20 percents during 2001-2003. Among those institutions, there were 10 Iranian IFIs and 6 Sudanese, a fact that supports the concept that IFIs working in fully Islamic banking systems are more profitable than those working in partially Islamic or in conventional ones.

4.3.12 ROE: Regional and Country-wise: At the

regional level, the Islamic financial institutions portfolio in the Middle East had the largest return on its shareholders' equity at 20.25 percent in 2003 although institutions working in that region usually pay income taxes for the governments of the countries in which they work. However, the large difference of asset size between IFIs in the Middle East and those in the GCC did not play a major role in increasing the difference between the ROE in the two regions due to several reasons including the stability of the exchange rate of the currencies of GCC countries that is characterized by long-term stability and the economic stability in that region.

4.4 Performance of Islamic Banks: The Case of Bank Islam Malaysia Berhad (BIMB)

Evaluation of bank performance is important for all parties: depositors, bank managers and regulators. In a competitive financial market and bank performance provides signal to depositors-investors whether to invest or withdraw funds from the bank. [14] Similarly, it flashes direction to bank managers whether to improve its deposit service or loan service or both, to improve its finance. Regulator is also interested to know the bank performance for its regulation purposes. Bank Islam Malaysia Berhad (BIMB) a name synonymous with Islamic banking in Malaysia continues to lead the way and to assume the role of trend setter for Islamic banking. [15]

The important underlying force that led to the establishment of this Islamic Bank in Malaysia was the elimination of *riba* (interest). *Tabung Haji* took the initiative to do business without using interest considered as being pre-determined rate of return to a deposit. *Tabung Haji* is an organization for the Muslims for taking care of pilgrims to Makkah. [16] It basically acts to facilitate the Muslims to perform their *Hajj* with the feeling of minimum financial burden. Its objective is to implement Muslim code of life (*Shari'ah*) in *Hajj* and all business transactions. All transactions in the conventional banks are based on interest or *riba* which is prohibited by Islam. *Tabung Hajj* wanted to get rid of *riba* (interest).

Islamic bank was sought as a solution to it. With the increase in Muslim population and awareness of Islamic values, there was a greater demand for Islamic bank and interest-free finance by Muslim consumers, traders, investors, and businessmen. Bank Islam Malaysia was established in July 1983 to meet these demands and challenges. [17] Since then, BIMB introduced and marketed various interest-free products such as *Wadiah* (savings account), *Akaun semasa* (current account), *Ijraa* (savings account), *Baiti* (Home Financing), General Investment Account, *Mudharabah Account*, Vehicle Financing, Bank Islam Card, Net banking and various other products. Bank's business has expanded over the years.

Its assets and deposits have increased from RM 3,609,456 million and RM 3,196,281 million respectively in 1996 to RM 14,60,5316 million and RM 14,38,6516 in 2006. The financing of loans and services increased to RM 8,50,1362 million in 2006. Therefore, the present study intends to study growth trends in performance of BIMB for the period 1996 to 2006. For better understanding of the progress and performance of BIMB, this section of the analysis has selected following performance indicators namely, deposits, financing of customers, reserves, assets, liabilities and profits. Using secondary data the performance of BIMB has been analysed during the period 1996-2006. [18]

4.4.1 Variations in Financial Performance Indicators of BIMB: 1996-2006: The results of variations in financial indicators of BIMB reveal the following facts. It could be indicated that assets recorded a greater level of mean value of RM 9827140; liabilities came second in order of mean value of RM 8811022, deposits took the third position in mean value of RM 8626313, financing of customers and reserves took the fourth and fifth order of mean value of RM 5276812 and RM 476874, while profit slipped down to the lowest order of mean value of RM 133642. Further, it is observed that the coefficient of variation analysis reveals that the reserves reported 62.09 percent of variation in BIMB during the reference period and this indicator recorded a higher level of fluctuation. In contrast, profit explained a 3.14 percent of fluctuation and it is said to be a lower order variations in BIMB. While liabilities reported second (i.e. 54.92 percent), financing of customers reported third (i.e. 48.2 percent), deposits and assets reported fourth and fifth in the order of fluctuation (i.e. 48.09 percent and 44.84 percent) during the study period.

It could be deducted from above discussion that the disparities of financial indicators represents that the assets recorded higher mean value and other financial indicators were left behind them, while the profit recorded a negative mean value. The analysis of coefficient of variations in profits recorded a very lower level of variations over a period of 11 years, whereas the remaining financial indicators exhibited greater variations. The negative mean value and very lower level of variation in profit during the reference periods was, mainly due to following reasons. The negative mean value was due to higher provisioning on non-performing financing of RM 648 million following the increase of non-performing financing level mainly attributed to BIMB Labuan Offshore Branch. The conversion of the subsidiary Bank Islam (L) Ltd., into an offshore branch of the Bank led to the adoption of stricter non-performing financing regulation as well as a more stringent risk management framework resulting in more prudent financial reporting of BIMB Labuan Offshore Branch activities.

4.4.2 Growth Trends in Financial Performance Indicators of BIMB: 1996-2006: For better understanding of the progress and performance of BIMB, growth index and exponential growth rate model were worked out for important financial indicators like assets, liabilities, financing of customers, reserves, deposits and profits. Trends in the growth of financial performance indicators of BIMB during 1996-

2006 indicate that the total deposits of BIMB recorded a near five-fold increase from RM 3,196,281 in 1996 to RM 14,386,516 in 2006. Though there was a gradual increase over the period, the increase was spectacular between 1998 and 2003. The average annual deposits over the period as a whole worked out to RM 8,626,313. It is interesting to note that the financing of customer in BIMB recorded a steady growth from RM 2,000,840 to RM 8,501,362 during 1996 to 2006. The financing of customers showed an increase of 109.21 percent in 2006 over 1996. There was a steady growth in the total reserves in BIMB from 1996 to 2006.

Further, the total amount of assets indicated that assets registered a rising trend during the period under review except in 2004 and 2006. There was a rising tendency from 1996 to 2003. It was 108.51 percent more in 2006 than in 2004. It was evident that liabilities of BIMB increased by 101.58 percent from RM 3,523,49 to RM 14,883,456 during the period under study. The liabilities of BIMB increased considerably except in 2004 and 2006. It is evident that reserves in BIMB increased by 83.10 percent from RM 123,702 to RM 115, 7840. The reserves in BIMB increased significantly from 1996 to 2004; during 2005 and 2006 the reserves of BIMB were lower.

The details of profits in BIMB explain that there were more fluctuating trends. It is noteworthy that there was a 72.84 percent increase from RM 24,959 to RM 75,262 during 2001 to 2004. During 1996 to 2000, the profits registered no linear trends (i.e. more fluctuation), whereas in 2005 and 2006, the profits had registered negative trends [i.e. RM (-) 507807 and RM (-) 1296789]. To evaluate the performance of BIMB, the major financial indicators were chosen and put into the analysis. The results indicated that the total deposits of the bank increased remarkably during 1996-2003 and 2005-2006.

It had registered an annual growth to reach RM 14386516 in 2006 from RM 3196281 in 1996 with an exponential growth rate of 7.36 percent per annum. In 2004, the deposit was RM 11268901; later on mobilization of deposits has increased. The second major financial indicators of financing of customers, showed an exponential growth rate of 7.04 percent per annum. The reason for this credit off-take was that the Bank had continued the strategy of focused marketing of credit for retail lending. The total assets and liabilities had an exponential growth rate of 6.85 and 12.19 percent per annum, respectively. The total reserves of BIMB indicated an average annual growth rate of 5.12 percent per annum, due to opening up of new branches thereby creating additional employment and implementation of various schemes. Net profit was obtained by deducting the total expenses from gross profit. Net profit showed the operational efficiency of the bank. The net profit of the bank under study recorded a remarkable increase during the period 2000-2004. The net profit of the BIMB during the study period had an exponential growth rate of 19.96 percent per annum. However, Bank Islam Malaysia suffered losses in the financial year 2004-2005 and 2005-2006.

A. Reasons for the Loss: 2004-2005 and 2005-2006: BIMB in November 2005 for the first time in its history reported a loss of RM 480 million (US$ 127,000,000), largely due to high non-performing loans from its Labuan [19] offshore unit. It closed its financial year with a total provision of RM 774 million, and total non-performing loans of RM 2.2 billion. The huge losses emerged when BIMB converted its Labuan office from a subsidiary to a branch in December 2004, and the affair had cast doubt on the effectiveness of Malaysia's regulatory and supervisory control of its banking system. Preliminary investigation showed that the problem rose due to the bank's poor credit evaluation and insufficient depth and breadth in processing loans and the bank's risk management frame being poorly established.

Huge non-performing loans were also detected mainly from the lending activities that were directed at the housing, car financing, and corporate financing markets without proper purposes. In October 2005, Malaysia business daily, 'The Edge' quoted BIMB CEO, Noorazman Aziz saying that Bank

Islam Malaysia Bhd has unveiled a comprehensive plan to tackle its whopping RM 2.2 billion (about US$ 600 million) worth of non-performing loans (NPLs). But little light was shed on how these bad loans arose in the first place, and more pertinently, who were responsible. Noorazman A. Aziz, the Bank's Managing Director and CEO narrowed down the cause to BIMB's Offshore Branch at Labuan. Noorazman confirmed news reports that some RM 450 million (about US$ 113 million) of bad loans were made to companies in Bosnia-Herzegovina and South Africa.

A July 2003 story published in the "Slobodna Bosna" magazine of Bosnia opined that BIMB is holding or has held deposits worth about Euro 300 million for the benefit of the Third World Relief Agency (TWRA). The story further suggested that these funds have been now made available to Bomsal, a Malaysian-Bosnian joint venture, for the construction of a toll highway. Bosmal itself had confirmed that it had received a financial facility from BIMB, for the highway as well as other development projects in Sarajevo. Market talk is that these companies were involved in construction and housing projects, and that more funds may need to be ploughed in to complete these projects before the borrowers can repay their debt. The Euro 300 million loans do not seem to appear anywhere in Bank Islam's books, and BIMB has refused to deny this assertion as well as to why the amount is way above Bank Islam's single customer lending limit.

B. Profits after the Loss: Bank Islam recorded a profit before tax of RM 165.8 million for the first six months ending 30th June 2007, compared with a loss of RM 43.2 million in the same period a year earlier. Revenue for the period totalled RM 467.8 million. This translated into a 17.6 percent return on shareholders' equity, compared with a negative return previously, the Bank's then Managing Director, Zukri Samat, said in a statement. [20] He said, "an efficient turnaround plan, which included strategic measures to grow new businesses and an aggressive loan recovery program, helped accelerate the bank's return to profitability after two years of losses. The effectiveness of these strategic changes has been amply demonstrated in the first half of our earnings. Forty percent of the RM 165.8 million profits came from operations, and the balance came from loan recoveries".

4.5 Conclusion

It could be deducted from above discussion that the Islamic Banks and Financial Institutions (IFIs) have become an integral part of the international finance and the regional bank industry. This clearly shows the widespread growth of IFIs since 1970s. IFIs have developed from individual trials into an integrated industry with its own standard, criteria, products and institutions. The success of IFIs can be summarised as follows:

1. Successes at the individual level including the high growth in attracting resources through investment and current accounts.
2. Success at the corporate level is represented by the tendency of several commercial and industrial companies to take decisions at the board level to be financed according to *Shari'ah* compliant modes.
3. Successes at the level of institutions offering Islamic banking and finance is reflected by the expansion of Islamic banking locally, regionally and internationally, a fact that makes conventional financial institutions display increased interest in delivering Islamic financial services with different structures and forms.

   Those institutions have established independent Islamic banks in terms of capital, financial statements and management. Other local conventional banks have gone towards full conversion to Islamic banking in order to meet the market needs.
4. IFIs have been able to create a new type of investors with positive thoughts and rational investment decisions that lead them to play an active role in the economic and

financial movement, instead of taking passive positions to get interests.

5. Banking is an activity where one is concerned with the management of other people's money. That is why bankers all over the world are conservative and cautious. Hence, the changes coming to the banking sector are usually slow. Furthermore, Islamic banking is just forty years old. It needs more time to mature and grow. Nevertheless, it may even be observed now that current scene of Islamic banking is dynamic in which changes within the system are continuously occurring. The need of the hour is to strengthen these emerging trends.

Further, financial performance of Islamic bank in case of Bank Islam Malaysia Berhad (BIMS) could be summarised as...It is observed that the variations in financial indicators represents that the assets recorded higher mean values and other financial indicators were left behind them, while the profit recorded a negative mean value. The analysis of coefficient of variations in profits recorded a very lower level of variations over a period of 11 years, whereas the remaining financial indicators exhibited greater variations. The negative mean value and very lower level of variations in profit during the reference period were mainly due to following reasons.

The negative mean value was due to higher provisioning on non-performing financing of RM 648 million following the increase of non-performing financing level mainly attributed to BIMB Labuan Offshore Branch. The conversion of the subsidiary Bank Islam (L) Ltd., into an offshore branch of the Bank led to the adoption of stricter non-performing financing regulation as well as a more stringent risk management framework resulting in more prudent financial reporting of BIMB Labuan Offshore Branch activities.

Further, it is also observed that the trend in all financial indicators during 1996-2006, registered considerable improvement, except in some years. The profit had registered negative trends particularly in 2005 and 2006. The growth rates of all the financial indicators reveal that liability registered the first order (12.09 percent per annum) during the years covered by the analysis viz. 1996-2006. In contrast, deposits followed next in order (i.e. 7.36 percent per annum), financing of customers represented third in order (i.e. 7.04 percent per annum), assets represented fourth in order (i.e. 6.85 percent per annum), reserves represented fifth in order (i.e. 5.12 percent per annum) and profits slid down to a negative growth (i.e. 19.96 percent per annum) of increasing trends in financial indicators of BIMB.

However, the growth rates of all the financial indicators of BIMB were statistically significant as shown in t values for the coefficient of B. Thus, from the above findings, it is found out that the all the financial indicators augmented rapidly during the study period. During 2005 and 2006, profit had registered negatively due to conversion of its Labuan office from a subsidiary to a branch in December 2004. An internal investigation about the negative growth rate pointed out that the bank had a poor credit evaluation method which lacked sufficient depth and breadth in processing loans.

Further, the Bank's risk management frame was not properly established, the huge non-performing loans also being detected mainly from the lending activities which were directed at housing, car financing and corporate financing markets without proper validation.

End Notes

1. Ghazali, A. et al. (eds.), An Introduction to Islamic Finance, Kuala Lumpur (Malaysia): Quill Publishers.
2. Institute of Islamic Banking and Insurance (1995), Encyclopaedia of Islamic Banking and Insurance, London: IIBI.
3. Islamic Cooperative Finance Ltd. and Salic Australia Pty. Ltd. are two other institutions in Australia.
4. Citi Islamic Investment Bank, Liquidity Management Centre, Gulf Finance House Commercial Bank, Noriba Bank, Unicorn.
5. Al Arafah Islamic Bank Limited, Islamic Finance and Investment Ltd., Oriental Bank Ltd. are other Islamic financial institutions in Bangladesh.

6. Bank Perkreditan Rakyat Sharia and Bait Maal Wat Tamwil are two other Islamic financial institutions in Indonesia. Besides, there are 88 micro Islamic banks in Indonesia.
7. Arab Finance Investment House and Lebanese Islamic Bank SAL are two other Islamic banks in Lebanon.
8. Al Aqsa Islamic Banks and Beit El Mal Holdings are two other Islamic banks in Palestine.
9. Al-Safa Islamic Banking, Doha Islamic, Doha Bank Branch and Investment House-Qatar are 3 other Islamic banks in Qatar.
10. Ibrahim Warde, Islamic Finance in the Global Economy, University Press, Edinburgh, 2000, p. 73.
11. Monzer Kahf, Clement M. Henry and Rodney Wilson (ed.), The Politics of Islamic Finance, Edinburgh University Press, 2004.
12. Arabia Monthly, April 1982, No. 8, p. 46.
13. Rad, Tourani A., Theoretical and Practical Aspects of the Interest-free Banking System, Netherlands Institute voor her Bank-en Effectenbedrijf, Amsterdam 1991, p. 92.
14. Akkas, Ali (1996), "Relative Efficiency of the Conventional and Islamic Banking System in Financing Investment", Unpublished Ph.D. Dissertation, Dhaka University.
15. Arif Mohammad, (1989), "Islamic Banking in Malaysia: Framework, Performance and Lesson", Journal of Islamic Economics, Vol. 2, No. 2.
16. Dirrar, E. Elbeid. (1996), "Economics and Financial Evaluation of Islamic Banking Operations: A Case of Bank Islam Malaysia 1983-1995". Unpublished paper, UIA.
17. Hassan, M. Kabir (1999), "Islamic Banking in Theory and Practice: The Experience of Bangladesh," Managerial Finance, Vol. 25, and Vol. 5: 60-113.
18. Based on Annual Reports of Bank Islam Malaysia Berhad.
19. Labuan is a Malaysian island off the Sabah Cost. Labuan is the Malaysian offshore financial services centre providing various tax initiatives.
20. Bank Islam Malaysia posts profit in first six months of financial year 2007.

5

Islamic Banking in India:
Issues and Constraints

5.1 Promotion of Interest-Free Banking and Finance in India

Interest-free banking and finance (IFBF), the more than trillion US\$ industry has shown resilience in the global recession of 2008, attracting the attention of even the countries with Muslim minority like UK and US. India is among those nations which are still hesitant to take the guardian's role for the interest-free banking and finance. IFBF is facing regulatory challenges in India. Policy makers themselves have different opinions regarding interest-free banking and finance. [1] Apart from the fact that it is Holy Scripture based, interest-free banking has comparative advantage with conventional system of banking. It should be examined and analyzed on the basis of purely economic, ethical, and welfare grounds. Western researchers who headed to look deeper into the interest-free banking have appreciated it. Like any evolving industry, interest-free banking and finance industry is also facing challenges and more fundamental and empirical researches are needed for smooth functioning and growth of the industry. However, researches suggest the wisdom of adopting and nurturing interest-free banking and finance rather than denouncing it.

5.1.1 Global Islamic Banking-An Overview: Several studies indicate a rapid growth in this sector. Estimating the size of this market is complicated by the rapid growth across several markets and untangling assets that are frequently included in both Islamic and conventional accounts within a single bank. Around 20 percent growth is reported by most of the studies which is higher than the growth of conventional banking system. Bahrain, Dubai/UAE and Kuala Lumpur are the main centres for Islamic banking and financial services due to their strong historical. Riyadh, Qatar, and Singapore is also not very much behind. London is aspiring to become the centre in Europe.

The market is currently most developed in Malaysia, Iran and the majority of countries that form the Gulf Co-operation Council (GCC). However, Islamic finance is moving beyond its historic boundaries in these countries into new territories both within and outside the Arab world.

5.1.2 Status in India: In India, Islamic banking is facing hurdles. There are efforts being made to establish a full fledged Islamic bank for the inclusion of the second largest population of the country which is reluctant of interest-based investments. Islamic financial institutions exist in India, in the form of non-banking financial institutions and Muslim Funds. [2] Bagsiraj in his comprehensive study on Islamic financial institutions in India has classified the Muslim non-banking financial institutions into four forms.

(a) *Muslim Financial Societies:* These are charitable trusts like Deoband Muslim Fund, Najibabad Muslim Fund etc. These societies are inoperable because they are based on charity and non-self sustainable institutions. There is a problem of managing the workforce and there is absence of standard system of operations; [3]

(b) *Muslim Financial Associations:* These are the associations made by individuals in various parts of the countries. Some of the famous associations are Barkat Association, Belgaum; Shantapuram Islamic Finance Corporation, Pattikadu; Interest-free Society, Pune; Millat Welfare Society, Faizabad; Mutual Benefit Group, Bhatkal. Financial Associations of Persons (FAPs) are unregistered, privately operated, smaller functional groups operating in mosques, educational institutions or markets, throughout the country, in mosques or *Anjumans.*

They have taken the form of smaller Bait-ul-Maals wherein *Zakah* funds are mobilized along with membership fees and donations, and interest-free *Qard-e-Hassan* loans are also extended. In the educational institutions they have taken the form of interest-free chit funds wherein groups of 25 to 30 staff members contribute a monthly fixed sum. [4]

(c) *Islamic Co-operative Credit Societies*: These societies are formed with 10-15 persons. These societies are providing assistance to the group members.

The problems with these societies are different regulations prevailing in different states; so a standard system could not be formed. Some of the societies are—The Patni Co-operative Credit Society Ltd., Surat, Bait-un-Nas'r Urban Co-operative Credit Society Ltd., Mumbai; Nehru College Staff Co-operative Credit Society Ltd., Hubli; and Al-Ansar Co-operative Credit Society Ltd., Hyderabad.

(d) *Islamic Investment and Financial Companies (IIFCs) of India* (Islamic NBFCs): Generally, most of the income is earned by IIFCs of India from *Ijara* i.e. leasing investments.

Hire-purchase and *Murabahah* i.e. mark-up pricing or cost plus finance which involves a contract in which a client wishing to purchase equipment or goods requests the company to purchase these items and resell them to him at a cost plus a reasonable profit payable on the terms agreed to between the parties, is another important source of IIFCs' earnings in India.

Musharakah, i.e. trust or joint project financing on profit and loss sharing basis are also employed as source of earnings, though on a lesser scale.

Investments in equity shares of the blue chip companies and in real estate or housing finance are other income earning avenues of IIFCs in India. Some of the famous companies are-Barkat Leasing and Financial Service Ltd., Mumbai; Al-Barr/Al-Baraka Finance House Ltd., Mumbai; Al-Ameen Islamic Finance and Investment Corporation Ltd., Bangalore; Seyad Shariat Finance Ltd., Tirunelveli; Al-Najeeb Milli Mutual Benefits Ltd., Najibabad. In the recent developments, there are some conventional financial institutions and banks who have introduced *Shari'ah* window to target the Muslims as their market in India. Some consultancies like TASIS and Taurus are working for investment guidance in *Shari'ah* compliant companies and financial Products. The Shariah Index established in BSE is responsible for screening *Shari'ah* compliant companies. [5]

5.1.3 Financial Freedom: Despite the prohibition of interest by four of the world's major religions (Judaism, Christianity, Hinduism, and Islam), today's international economic system is based on interest. However, efforts are going on to replace the conventional interest-based banking system with the interest-free banking and finance. Apart from religious dimension, the case against interest has been examined by many researchers.

The major argument in favour of interest-free banking is that it brings discipline in the economy, thus reducing the possibility of financial crises. As excessive lending is one of the major contributors to the financial crises, the profit and loss sharing system ensures a more responsible behaviour from the bankers and the depositors. Overall, interest-free banking and finance aims for socio-economic justice and full employment. The four universally-cherished humanitarian goals—needs' fulfilment, full employment, equitable distribution and economic stability, —are the goals of interest-free banking and finance also. [6]

5.1.4 Virtual Debt Slaves: Many economists believe that today's economy is "debt-based", meaning that virtually all money is supplied into the economy as a debt owed to the corporate banking system. As a consequence, of virtually all our money coming into existence as a debt, we see the indebtedness of people, families and countries growing daily. Money reformers believe that the present debt-based system perpetrates debt slavery, and this is destructive for society, the environment and the planet. Money reformers believe this debt-based money supply is the big issue which governs all the issues. Money reformers advocate that the virtual monopoly of money creation must be removed from the corporate banking system and we work to establish debt-free money. Profit and loss sharing and other tools of interest-free banking can go a long way in reforming the economy.

5.2 Reasons for Interest-free Banking in India

Islamic finance (Interest-free finance: used interchangeably) is ultimately governed by ethics and passion for human welfare. Morality is imbedded in the rules, through the prohibition of production and exchange of goods harmful to life and environment. In addition, contracts that do not carefully balance the interests of both parties and those that make pure risk, a subject of trade are not permissible. Speculation and gambling–a feature of the current economic system–are prohibited in any form. Even the simple financial instruments have become so complex to resemble speculation and gambling. The Islamic banking seems to be synonymous with ethical banking. This covers all aspects of economy like stock exchanges, financial services and different sectors of the economy.

5.2.1 Increased Flow of Funds: Interest-free banking and finance has potential of attracting huge inflow of foreign direct investment (FDI) and foreign institutional investors (FIIs) from Gulf nations which are reluctant to invest on credit terms. It has the potential of attracting trillion Dollar equity finance from Gulf Cooperation Council (GCC) countries. Significant investments are also expected from countries involved in interest-free banking and finance like UK, China, Singapore, Malaysia and Japan. There are at least four reasons why an interest-free system may be expected to promote economic stability discussed below. [7]

A. Investment: Many economists believe that debt financing is a major factor destabilizing investment in capitalist economies. Their argument is that a system of short-term financing of long-term capital assets has inherent limitations. That is, cash flows expected from such assets extended longer than the terms of debt contracted to acquire them. Under such a system of financing, debt is repaid when due by issuance of new debt, i.e. refinancing is an on-going process. When expectations about future cash-flows and interest rates are fulfilled, refinancing is easily achieved, and contractual interest obligations are easily met from cash flows generated by the assets. But if expectations take a wrong turn (either interest rates go up or current cash flows go down) refinancing becomes difficult. Attempts then to acquire cash by selling assets bring asset values to a level below their past prices, or even below their current cost of reproduction. This brings investment to a halt, and brings down income and employment. Similar is the Henry Simon's view that, "the danger of economic instability could be minimised if no resort were made to borrowing, particularly short-term borrowing and if all investments were held in the form of equity".

B. Speculation: The speculative demand for money, which is one source of instability in the Keynesian system, would be significantly reduced in an interest-free economy because the abolition of interest would drive out the speculation on interest bearing assets. Interest bearing loans would no longer be available to fuel cumulative speculation. This is quite significant, as speculators would be confined to their own funds–no funds would be coming to them on profit sharing basis, unless the suppliers of such funds themselves want to speculate.

C. Corporate Finance: Corporate finance propounds that an increase in debt financing (as opposed to equity-financing) of a firm increases its risk of insolvency and magnifies the relative fluctuations in its earnings (net of interest). Firms that have higher debt-equity ratio are more likely to face financial collapse during cyclical downturns because their fixed interest payments must be met in the short-run.

5.2.2 International Finance: Minor change in interest rate differentials induces movement of funds over countries. Profit rate differentials in short-run does not have the same destabilizing effect as equity participants entail long-term commitments that cannot be profitably be undone in response to minor change in profit rate differentials. Hence, equity financing is intrinsically more stable than the one based on interest. After the 'global crisis' and bankruptcy of financial giants in 2008, there is a quest for alternate model of economic system. The strict obligations of interest-free institutions prevent the financial and economic enterprises from bankruptcy which has its roots in a moral failure that leads to exploitation and corruption. Even the calls for market liberalization, deregulation and philosophy of non interference with financial markets have immoral dimensions. [8]

5.2.3 Interest-free Micro Finance: Micro finance is today's buzzword. But like every evolving industry, it is facing challenges and problems. High interest rates, coercive collection methods and corrupt and unethical practices are among the most cited problems this industry is facing. The reasons of existence of this industry are quoted, as to provide low income population, an access to credit and thereby aid in poverty alleviation. Can this social objective be achieved through asocial means? To realize the high end social objectives of micro finance, a holistic approach must be taken. Apart from earning by doing well, the ethical and moral practices must be an integral part of micro finance.

A movement is going on in the world for interest-free banking and finance. All four major religions of the world (Christianity, Judaism, Islam, and Hinduism) have prohibited interest. There is a strong rationale behind the prohibition of interest. A system based on interest is prone to many unwanted consequences like unequal distribution of wealth, exploitation of poor and weaker sections of society and emergence of debt slaves. Micro finance can act as a growth vehicle for India as 'Real India lives in villages'. It can foster the development of entrepreneurship in rural and sub-urban areas, reduce the migration to urban areas causing over-populated cities.

This also goes in line with the PURA model of A.P.J. Abdul Kalam. Investment in social causes (social finance) needs a holistic approach. So why not an interest-free model of micro finance be implemented and practiced, which other than having its roots in scriptures has many advantages like responsible behaviour of both the microfinance institutions (MFI) and borrowers and ethical practices. As the interest-free model of micro finance is based on profit and loss sharing (PLS) basis, given the inherent conflict between socio-economic objectives and profit motives, the MFI industry should think of alternative models. Interest-free models of micro finance are a better option.

5.2.4 Entrepreneurship Development: Interest-free banking and finance go a long way in developing and promoting entrepreneurship in the economy. The inspirational entrepreneurs who do not have sufficient collateral can get the help through interest-free finance, as Islamic banking does not allow giving loans on interest. The investors have either the option of giving Qardhe Hasana (interest-free loans) or forming any type of partnership (Madharaba, Musharaka). The contract must be free of Riba (interest), Gharar (excessive risk), and Mysir (Gambling). Islamic banking promotes innovation in the financing forms and types of products.

5.3 Growth of Islamic Banking in India

India has no enough reasons to avoid the exponential growth of Islamic banking worldwide. The growth in this sector is more than the growth of normal banking system. Why should it not promote Islamic banking if it is promising sustainable development with many other advantages. The proponents of the interest-free banking and finance have to prove the benefits by empirical data. The level of discourse would be at a new height if empirical studies prove the comparative advantage of Islamic banking.

A. Financial Inclusion of Muslims: The 2001 census of India concludes that Muslims constitute 13.4 percent of the total population of the nation, which makes it the third largest Muslim country after Indonesia and Pakistan. Economic marginalization of Muslim community in India can be dealt with through the promotion of interest-free banking and finance which may be welcomed by the Muslim community to a large extent. Access to bank credit by Muslims is only 4.3 percent which is very low as compared to their share of population.

B. Opponents of Islamic Finance: Those who oppose Islamic banking and finance argue that it targets only one section of the society. This is neither right theoretically nor practically. Studies in UK, Malaysia and other countries indicate the popularity of Islamic banking among non-Muslims due to its ethical or reliability dimensions. The religious dimension is not an important factor in determining the usage of services of Islamic banks. [9] Even the marketers do not position themselves it as a niche market meant only for Muslims. Those who argue that an economic system based on religion cannot be propagated in a secular nation, are at the risk of missing the advantages of joining the elite first movers.

5.4 Multi-dimensional Approach of Islamic Finance in India

The Islamic finance for its successful journey in the Indian market should focus on three important dimensions. These dimensions have to be kept in view when we are planning and discussing about the operation, functioning and contributive role of Islamic finance in India. First, India's life revolves in rural areas. As per the recent data, 72 percent of Indian population resides in rural areas to which the prevailing financial services are not reachable. This huge population, which is not provided with the satisfactory and just services by the present day banking and financial system, should be the first dimension where Islamic finance (industry) needs to focus. It is a well-known fact that the major occupations of the rural population include agriculture, husbandry, cattle breeding and other small and marginal agro-based industries. These small occupations and industries are falling sick because of unavailability of financial support.

It has been a tragedy that wherever the financial support is made available, the customers are pulled into debt traps resulting in suicides and other socio-economical problems. Hence, to provide better financial support for the rural population should be one of the main objectives of Islamic finance (industry) in India. Secondly, the Indian sub-continent happens to be the habitat for around 160 million Muslims, the second largest figure in any nation witnessing historic relation of India with Islamic finance. The Indian Muslims own ₹ 50 billion as annual inevitable resources that are not utilised.

But according to the Sachar Committee Report, 70 percent of Muslims keep themselves away from playing any direct or indirect role in the Indian financial sector. The main reason behind is the prevalence of 'interest' (which is prohibited and termed as a major sin in Islam) in this sector. Owing to this single reason, they are excluded from having a crucial role in the nation's growth and development. Therefore, Islamic finance can become a ray of hope for this section of society and may help in taking this community to the mainstream to contribute to the national development. And from the religious point of view also, it will keep them away from woes of interest-based financial services, strictly prohibited in Islam.

Thirdly, according to a report of the Investment Commission of India, major sectors like infrastructure has an opportunity of US$ 427 billion as investment, services sector around, US$ 143 billion, manufacturing sector, US$ 229 billion, knowledge economy, US$ 38 billion and natural resources, an opportunity of US$ 35 billion as investment for the next five years. While planning to accumulate this huge capital—and going for debt both from internal and external sources, which could be a risky job and might result in an enchanced debt trap—Islamic finance can play a vital role. This would eliminate and clear the misunderstandings about the Islamic finance that it is a religious finance focused on a particular section i.e. Muslims and has nothing to do with national development.

Islamic finance with its products like micro finance would provide satisfactory services to the daily wage workers, farmers and other BPL families. Towards growing population in urban cities, Islamic finance can come up with innovative products and satisfactory services in the sectors like capital market, insurance, mutual fund, retail market, trading loans, real estate and small infrastructural development projects.

At national level, there are many opportunities in the form of long-term infrastructural development that are expected in future and have to be cracked with full plan.

It is to be noted that constituting a co-operative society, a trust as domestic venture capital fund and foreign venture capital funds registered with SEBI, Islamic insurance business, an Islamic window in a conventional bank, to carry on *Shari'ah* financing activities is permissible within the existing laws and regulations. Hence, apart from making efforts for changes in the laws, the Islamic financial system can also be introduced easily by starting what is permissible within the extant laws.

A. Foremost Challenge: The first and foremost challenge is of legal issues. The entry of Islamic finance in the form of banks and NBFCs require changes in the prevailing laws in Indian financial and capital market, particularly the Banking Regulation Act of 1949 under which all financial institutions are regulated and monitored.

The Working Group constituted by RBI in its report concluded that there are appropriate amendments required in Banking Regulation Act, 1949 and a separate rules and regulation will have to be formed to permit the business of Islamic banking in India. It depends upon the ability of the Islamic finance (industry) how it convinces the Government of India and lawmaking body to amend the prevailing laws or to introduce the new law and act in its favour.

B. Government and its Policies: The second challenge is the government body and its policies. India is known as the largest democracy all over the world. Being large, it is uncertain and ever-changing, and also carries slow procedures with corrupt system. With the changing governments, most of the policies adopted change. The new government designs new policies, which may or may not support the decisions of the previous government. Therefore, these features may have an effect on the government's decision on Islamic finance and banking in India as seen from the past.

C. Model and Structure: India is a multicultural society. It has a different identity due to its different demographical, geographical, socio-political and economical diversity. Therefore, the existing models of Islamic finance in the GCC, European region and even in the Asian nations like Pakistan, Indonesia and Malaysia are not fully feasible of being implemented in the Indian market. Most of the models are either designed in the Muslim majority nations or in the trade-based economy, whereas in India, the majority are non-Muslims and the economy of India is production based or is agro-industrial based. Therefore, either these existing models have to be modified on its major part or the experts have to design a new model of Islamic finance which best suits Indian market. This is the fourth challenge that Islamic finance (industry) is going to face.

D. Research and Development: In India, very limited literature has been written on Islamic finance in Indian perspective, specifically in regional languages. The limited literature available does not discuss the Islamic finance in India in detail. The second reason is that very few products of Islamic finance are available in India. This variety of products that are available in the market cannot satisfy the huge population of customers. Therefore, there is a need to have enough literature and innovative, feasible, profitable and much diversified products in India. To develop such a huge literature and variety of products that can teach and satisfy the rural and urban customers at a time, Islamic finance in India needs research and development (R&D) centres throughout the nation. The task of R&D with respect to literature, processes, products, market and functions has to be carried out with rapidity. This is the fifth challenge for Islamic finance (industry) in India.

E. Qualitative Human Resource: The sixth challenge is the qualitative human resources (HR). The Islamic financial institutions require both qualitative and well-trained professionals to meet the competition in market. Without qualitative HR, the road to success may not be possible. Hence, there rises a new task for this industry to teach and train the youngsters on the required areas of Islamic finance.

5.5 Issues and Constraints in Establishing Islamic Banks in India

Before discussing the issues and constraints of establishing Islamic banks in India, it is relevant to point out the experience of certain modern secular countries in accommodating Islamic banks and Islamic financial products in their banking system. The experiences of these countries would be an eye opener for the Indian Government in deciding about permitting the functioning of Islamic banks in India.

5.5.1 Britain: Muslims in Britain are estimated to be around 1.8 million–some 3 percent of the population. They make up around 3,40,000 households. There are a further half million Muslim visitors each year spending nearly £600 million. A rough estimate suggests that the UK's Muslims have, in total, savings of approximately £1 billion. The British regulatory authorities felt that it would have been an invidious form of social exclusion for regulation to have prevented the development of financial products which conformed to the Muslim population's religious beliefs, and therefore to have condemned them to a position where their religious beliefs prevented them from accessing financial services.

The UK Financial Services Authorities has been concerned to avoid this. The importance of preventing this form of exclusion from the benefits of the financial system lay behind the work which led to the establishment in August 2004 of the first wholly *Shari'ah* compliant retail bank in Europe or the US, the Islamic Bank of Britain. The UK Financial Services authorities resolved a number of regulatory issues, the most problematic of which was the treatment of Islamic deposits. By settling this, and other issues, they have not only enabled the Islamic Bank of Britain (now with seven branches) to be set up, but have also enabled already established banks, including some of the traditional high street banks, to offer *Shari'ah* compliant products. All these developments represent a major move towards financial inclusion–as well as to the ending of a barrier between communities which, like other barriers, need to be eliminated.

Commenting on this development, Howard Davies, Chairman, UK Financial Services Authority said, "Although the FSA has no statutory duty to promote financial inclusion, we are very pleased to have been able to make such a substantial contribution to this end". [10] Mr. Howar Davies further stated, "it is important that we show, we were able to accommodate Islamic banking practices alongside traditional non-Islamic banking, for reasons both of principle and of practical importance. We are very conscious of the rapid growth of Islamic banking worldwide over the last 25 years. London has a successful record as a trading centre for Islamic products: LME *mudaraba* trading and *sukuks* are examples, as well as the established *Shari'ah* compliant activities of major western investment banks.

In March this year the FSA authorised the European Islamic Investment Bank–as its name suggests a wholly *Shari'ah* compliant wholesale Islamic bank. It is reasonable to regard London as a centre for a full range of *Shari'ah* compliant wholesale products–an important objective if London is to retain its international character." One of the most important issues resolved by the FSA is that of Islamic deposits. The UK legal definition of a deposit is, "a sum of money paid on terms under which it will be repaid either on demand or in circumstances agreed by the parties". In other words, money placed on deposit must be capital certain. For a simple non-interest bearing account, there is no problem.

The bank safeguards the customer's money and returns it when the terms of the account require it to do so. However, with a savings account there is a potential conflict between UK law, which requires capital certainty, and *Shari'ah* law, which requires the customer to accept the risk of a loss in order to have the possibility of a return. Islamic banks resolve this problem by offering full repayment of the investment but informing the customer how much should be repayable to comply with the risk-sharing formulation. This allows customers to choose not to accept full repayment if their religious convictions dictate otherwise.

5.5.2 United States of America: Muslim social scientists and researchers have spent a great deal of time trying to determine the number of Muslims in the United States. Most accept the estimate of from 6 million to 8 million, that is to say at least 5 million people in North America claim Islam as their religion and/or practice. What is represented in this report is based on estimates made in 1991, the World Almanac reports that Muslim in the United States number approximately 5,220, 00. In many cases, existing US law is broad enough to encompass *Shari'ah* compliant structures.

Practitioners create products that simultaneously satisfy the demands of secular and religious law, in much the same way as they must look to the law of two or more jurisdictions in structuring a cross-border transaction. This is possible because, in general, the secular law in the United States is silent with respect to matters of religion and because the common law tradition is one of flexibility and adaptation. Thus, for example, bankruptcy remote special purpose vehicles created under US law have been used in both conventional securitization transactions and in *ijara*-based commercial real estate financings. That in the latter case the structure is used to comply with a religious law is irrelevant in the eyes of the secular law.

As in other jurisdictions, two types of Islamic financing vehicles are commonly used in the United States: *ijara* and *murabaha*. The first major milestones for the provision of Islamic retail banking services in the United States were two interpretive letters issued by the Office of the Comptroller of the Currency—both letters were issued in the late 1990s in response to proposals submitted by the United Bank of Kuwait. Although federal banking regulators have provided little formal guidance with respect to Islamic financial products, the Office of the Comptroller of the Currency (the OCC) issued two key interpretive letters in 1997 and 1999 concerning products designed to be *Shari'ah* compliant.

In each case, the OCC looked beyond the form of the transaction to its economic substance and concluded that the product was "functionally equivalent to or a logical outgrowth of" secured lending and therefore permissible under existing banking law. The 1997 approval involved a residential net lease-to-own home finance product (*ijara wa iqtina*) proposed by the New York branch of United Bank of Kuwait. The program involved a home buyer identifying a property he or she wanted and approaching the bank for financing.

The bank and the home buyer would then simultaneously enter into a purchase agreement and a net lease agreement. The bank would fund the purchase price and take legal title of the property. It would then lease the property "as is" to the home buyer. Once the home buyer has paid the final lease instalment, he or she acquires the title to the property.

The terms of the lease require the home buyer-lessee to maintain the property and pay expenses that an owner-purchaser would ordinarily pay. In case of a material default under the lease, the bank's remedies against the home buyer for non-payment would be similar to those available to a lender on a traditional non-recourse mortgage, i.e. the bank could sell the property at an auction to recover the money owed under the lease.

The 1999 approval involved a proposal by the United

Bank of Kuwait to offer certain *murabaha*-based financing products. These products were designed to permit the bank to acquire an item of commercial inventory or equipment or a parcel of real estate and then resell that property to the bank's customer on an instalment basis at cost plus a mark-up. In each case, the bank's customer would identify the property to be financed. Because the purchase and sale transactions occurred simultaneously, the OCC took the view that the bank would be acting as a "riskless principal" in such transactions and that there were therefore permissible activities. [11]

Commercial banks in the United States are generally restricted from owning real property, apart from their own premises and parcels they may have acquired through foreclosure proceedings. The latter must generally be sold as soon as practicable. The prudential regulatory restriction against banks owning real estate is a perfect illustration of a secular rule that may fetter the free exercise of religion.

Some in the industry had predicted that such regulatory restrictions would prevent the use of *ijara* or *murabaha* in the real estate context. The OCC's subsequent approval of these *Shari'ah*-compliant products proved those predictions wrong. Thomas C. Baxter Jr., Executive Vice-President and General Counsel, Federal Reserve Bank of New York is of the opinion [12] that the "approval granted by OCC demonstrates the type of creative thinking necessary to accommodate a religious practice not generally considered when the banking laws were first drawn up.

The restrictions on bank ownership of real estate were put in place not to penalize or prevent Islamic institutions from operating but to address risks associated with real estate speculation. By looking to the economic substance of the transaction, the OCC was able to recognize that the risks incurred by the proponents of these products were not the same risks the statutes sought to curtail. As banking supervisors, we ought to be prepared to reach similar accommodations, while continuing to insist that financial institutions operate in a safe and sound manner."

This flexible approach has fostered notable development of Islamic banking services in the United States. Although estimates of the potential size of this market vary widely, it is clear from the recent domestic growth of these services that significant demand exists for these products. HSBC, University Bank in Ann Arbor, Michigan, and Devon Bank of Chicago all now offer Islamic banking products in the United States. There are also several non-bank mortgage and finance companies offering these services. Freddie Mac and Fannie Mae have purchased *Shari'ah*-compliant mortgages from a number of these providers, supplying crucial liquidity that has enabled these Islamic financial institutions to originate additional mortgages. SHAPE Financial Corp. has developed a number of proprietary *Shari'ah*-compliant products that are currently sold through University Bank in Ann Arbor, Michigan.

These include an *ijara*-based mortgage substitute and a profit-sharing deposit product. SHAPE's experience in gaining approval of its profit-sharing deposit illustrates that not all regulatory obstacles to Islamic finance have been overcome. In 2002, SHAPE approached the Federal Deposit Insurance Corporation (the FDIC), which insures deposits in commercial banks up to US$ 100,000 per depositor, with a proposal to create a deposit product whose returns would fluctuate based on the offering bank's profits or losses. The "catch" was that the deposit could decline in value. According to SHAPE, the FDIC was not prepared to countenance a deposit that could lose value. [13]

Consequently, SHAPE redesigned the product to eliminate downside risk. Instead of a true profit-and-loss sharing deposit product, it became a profit-sharing deposit, whose capital is guaranteed by the bank but whose returns fluctuate based on the profits of the bank overall or on the profits of specific operations. If there is no gross profit, the deposit pays no yield. From the above discussion, we can infer that the United States has given room for Islamic products in the banking sector.

5.5.3 Singapore: Among rich industrial nations with more than a million population, Singapore has the highest portion of its population that is Muslim. In Singapore, Muslims constitute 18.4 percent of the population. Singapore cannot ignore the importance of growth of Islamic finance and therefore had added Islamic financial products to the suite of conventional financial products that Singapore already offers. The depth and liquidity of the Singapore market is a source of strength. Singapore is a leading player in the Real Estate Investment Trusst (REITs) industry and REIT's property based funds are forms of financial instruments that can easily be packaged to be *Shari'ah*-compliant. Thus far, three Islamic property funds have already been set up in Singapore, with funds of over US US$ 1.35 billion earmarked for investment in Asian real estate. The following are some of the initiatives being taken to facilitate the growth of Islamic financial market.

Singapore has been systematically reviewing its policies to ensure that Islamic finance is not disadvantaged vis-à-vis conventional finance. Singapore Government's approach is to level the playing field and ensure the neutrality of rules applicable to conventional and Islamic financing wherever possible. As the prudential objectives of adequate capitalization and liquidity, appropriate management of risks and concentration, corporate governance and controls are largely similar between Islamic financial activities and conventional financial services. Singapore's existing regulatory framework, with suitable refinements, has facilitated the development of Islamic finance in Singapore. Where there are specific risks or impediments, rules have been refined to address these specific areas. Islamic banks, *Takaful and retakaful* companies or Islamic capital markets players interested to operate in Singapore need not apply for a separate category of license, i.e. the same licensing regime as that for conventional financial institutions will apply.

Monetary Authority of Singapore (MAS), the Central

Bank of Singapore has fine tuned its rules to allow all banks in Singapore to offer *Murabaha* financing which is a common structure in trade finance.

Previously, MAS regulations imposed broad restrictions on banks against conducting non-financial activities. MAS has now exempted *Murabaha* financing, which requires the banks to purchase goods at its customer's request and to sell the goods to the customer at a mark-up. Later banks in Singapore were also allowed to offer *Murabaha* investment products. The exemption is granted in recognition of the product's fundamental characteristics as a financial product.

In the area of taxation, given the nature and structure of Islamic financial products, they tend to attract more taxes than their conventional counterparts. The Minister of Finance announced several changes in the budget for 2005 and again in the budget for 2006 to level the playing field for Islamic transactions. In 2005, the Ministry of Finance waived the imposition of double stamp duties on Islamic transactions involving real estate and accorded the same concessionary tax treatment on income from Islamic bonds that are afforded to conventional bonds.

In the 2006 budget announcement, Income tax and GST (Goods and Services Tax) applications on some Islamic products were further clarified.

The Ministry of Finance has adopted an important approach to align the tax treatment of Islamic contracts with the treatment of conventional financial contracts that they are economically equivalent to. Hence, the tax treatment of three *Shari'ah*-compliant financial concepts has been harmonized with the conventional products to ensure a level playing field with respect to tax. In addition, for *sukuk*, remission will be granted on stamp duty on immovable property, incurred under a *sukuk* structure, which is in excess of that chargeable in the case of an equivalent conventional bond issue.

Over the last 2 to 3 years, a number of Islamic products and services have emerged in Singapore. This includes the launch of *Shari'ah*-compliant real estate funds and Islamic securities funds. The FTSE SGX Asia 100 *Shariah* Index was launched in February 2006. The Index, made up of 100 stocks in the Asia-Pacific that are *Shari'ah*-compliant, will be used as a basis for the creation of financial products such as exchange-traded funds and over-the-counter trading instruments. In addition, Singapore is also witnessing the growth of Islamic trade financing, Islamic deposits and *retakaful* capacity.

Mr. Heng Swee Keat, Manging Director of Monetary Authority of Singapore is of the opinion [14] that the Islamic finance industry in Singapore has developed much faster, especially in recent years. He has also in a speech declared, "the Monetary Authority of Singapore (MAS) has conducted a review of the regulatory framework in relation to Islamic banking. Some jurisdictions have a separate Islamic banking regulatory framework that exists in parallel to their conventional framework, while others have regulated both Islamic and conventional banking within a common regulatory framework. As many of the supervisory processes and prudential measures are common to both conventional and Islamic banking activities, MAS has opted to accommodate Islamic banking within the existing supervisory framework for banks. MAS will not be making any fundamental changes to their supervisory framework, but will refine the rules along the way to facilitate the development of Islamic finance".

The financial community in Singapore is excited by the recent growth and developments in Islamic banking and finance. The Monetary Authority of Singapore is committed to supporting this development. Singapore, as an international financial centre, has a full suite of Islamic financial products that can meet the needs of banks and investors.

5.5.4 Sri Lanka: The majority of Sri lanka's 19.5 million populations is Buddhist (77 percent), while Muslims constitute about 8.5 percent of the population. Sri Lanka is one of the few non-Islamic countries to have legislated for Islamic banking. The revised Banking Act No. 30 of 1988, as amended in 2005, allows both commercial banks and specialized banks to operate on a *Shari'ah*-compliant basis, including, "the acceptance of a sum of money in any manner or form from any person for a fixed period of time for investment in a business venture of the bank on the basis that profits or losses of the venture will be shared with the person from whom such money is accepted in a manner determined at the time the money is accepted." This landmark legislation came in after years of intensive discussions and lobbying by Amana Investments, the pioneer Islamic service provider in the country, with the Central Bank of Sri Lanka. Islamic banking has been a long-cherished need among Sri Lanka's Muslims since the creation of market awareness in 1997, when Amana entered the market as the pioneering Islamic financial institution offering *Shari'ah*-compliant deposit and financing products.

There have been other attempts at village and provincial levels to create Islamic fund-type operations, but their success has been limited due to, among other reasons, their being unregistered entities with little professionalism and the absence of a profit motive. Of late, the Ceylinco Group has formed a company that offers PLS-based products to the market. The market for Islamic financial products is dominated by Amana Investments, with others such as Muslim Commercial Bank, Ceylinco Profit Sharing, People's Leasing Company and First Global Investments, also operating. Amana has led the market both in terms of creating awareness and providing *Shari'ah*-compliant financial solutions.

Whilst the group was able to obtain early regulatory approval to operate its *Takaful* insurance business, the regulatory approval for a banking license has taken well over seven years, as it involved fundamental changes to the Banking Act. Amana is now at the head of the queue for a licence to operate as a fully fledged Islamic commercial bank. Following the new legislation, some of the existing conventional banks are expected to open Islamic banking windows with a view to preventing their Muslim customers from migrating to Islamic banks. It is also possible that the market might see a few new entrants to Islamic banking, although the Central Bank has upped the minimum capital requirements for licensing substantially.

The size of the Islamic market is estimated at around US$ 500 million-US$ 600 million. The regulators are becoming alive to the growing Islamic market segment, both local and global, and the global developments and trends in Islamic banking. Some of the key challenges they face in this regard include developing appropriate mechanisms to regulate Islamic banks, facilitating inter-bank transactions and developing relevant inter-bank and treasury instruments for the investment of surplus funds by Islamic banks. Further relevant changes to the fiscal and legislative environments will soon be necessary to facilitate Islamic banking transactions. Yet another challenge facing the industry is the competency gap in human resources, both at the regulatory and market levels. Islamic bankers and *Shari'ah* scholars are scarce resources and are critical success factors to the industry's future growth and development. All in all, Sri Lanka is an emerging market and the scope for Islamic banking looks both positive and exciting.

5.5.5 Proposal for Introduction of Islamic Banks in India: It is observed that Islamic banking and finance is an innovation of the world in present times. India has largely remained on the outer fringe of the development of Islamic banking and finance. Except for those countries where Islamic banking is being introduced on an economy-wide scale, most Islamic banking institutions have been established in the private sector. In view of the on-going processes of liberalization and globalization, restructuring of the banking sector is long overdue. Introduction of Islamic banking in the private sector shall boost private commercial banking in India.

India has lately adopted the policy of opening up the banking sector and many foreign banks are now operating in India. India should learn from the experiences of Singapore and could invite more foreign capital to the country if it allows not only foreign Islamic banks but also conventional commercial banks to open Islamic windows as have been done in several European countries. The Indian Banks Association (IBA) has also appealed for allowing Islamic banking in India. IBA Chairman M.B.N. Rao has gone on record saying, "it (Islamic banking) is an idea, whose time has come. The IBA will study the concept, but will wait for the regulatory framework by the RBI to run it".

In view of the fact that Islamic financial techniques are not based on interest, Islamic banking has a special relevance for micro credit institutions in satisfying financial needs of weaker sections of the Indian society. Indian banks are regulated by the Indian Banking Regulation Act, 1949, The Reserve Bank of India Act, 1935, The Negotiable Instruments Act and Cooperative Societies Act, 1866. None of these laws admit the possibility of an interest free bank. Hence, these laws will have to be amended significantly to admit such a possibility and to evolve a suitable system of regulation and control.

The following sections in the Banking Regulation Act have to be taken into consideration while amending the Act or enacting a new legislation permitting Islamic banks in India— *Section 21 of the Banking Regulation Act* requires payment of interest on saving bank account deposits. This section should be amended to permit *Al Wadiah. Section 21 of the Banking Regulation Act* disallows products like Mudarabah (trust financing) where the bank can invest the money in equity funds (in India, equity exposure is determined by a separate set of rules), and the client has complete freedom in the management. *Sections 5, 6 of the Banking Regulation Act* indicate the forms of business a banking company can undertake, and does not allow any kind of profit-sharing and partnership contract like Musharakah (for project finance and SME credit)—the basis of Islamic Banking. *Section 9 of the Banking Regulation Act* prevents the bank from owning any sort of immovable property other than for private use.

This section thus prevents banks from introducing *Ijarah*

(leasing) under which Islamic banks finance equipment, building or other facility for the client against agreed rental while owning the asset. Besides the usual curbs on acquiring immovable property, under the current Indian Laws offering Islamic banking products, many not are bankable due to stamp duty, central sales tax and state tax laws that will apply depending on the nature of the transfer. In markets like the UK, there is separate law that makes it possible to launch Islamic banking products. Singapore and Sri Lanka have amended their Banking Regulation Act to accommodate Islamic banking products. Singapore has also amended its taxation laws to solve this problem. The Banking Regulation Act even disallows an Indian bank from floating a subsidiary abroad to launch such products, or offering these through a special window. Thus, in India Islamic banking experiment is impossible without a new law (or multiple amendments to the Banking Regulation Act).

One way of amending the laws would be to maintain the current legislation with regard to conventional banks but to specifically enact laws applicable to interest-free Islamic banks. The new legislation will have to expressly allow the regulatory authority the ability to deem a bank capable of interest-free operations. Once that authority has deemed a bank capable of interest-free operations, current legislation will no longer apply and a new set of laws will apply. Those new laws will govern their activities and subject them to the regulatory body. The regulatory body would assist in establishing and enforcing auditing and accounting standards, ensuring transparency in the dealings of interest-free banks and ensuring compliance with liquidity standards.

The regulatory body, in conjunction with industry experts, could also look into some form of deposit insurance for accountholders and some form of a rating agency to judge the efficiency and managerial competency of the newly-developing interest-free banks helping to ensure the stability of the parallel interest-free banking network being set up.

Therefore, it could be concluded that at a time when India has adopted the policy of throwing open the banking sector to foreign players, permitting Islamic banks and Islamic windows in commercial banks would attract more foreign capital to the country.

End Notes

1. A Growth Model for Islamic Banking: Mckinsey Quarterly, October 2005.
2. Bagsiraj, M.I. (2002), Islamic Financial Institutions of India: Progress, Problems and Prospects, Scientific Publishing Centre, King Abdul Aziz University.
3. Issues in International financial Crisis: From an Islamic Perspective (2009), Islamic Economic Research Centre, King Abdul Aziz University.
4. Monzer Kahf (1999), Islamic Banks at the Threshold of Third Millennium, Thunderbird International Business Review, Volume 41, Issue 4-5, pp. 445-460.
5. Uzair, Mohammad (1978), Interest-free Banking, Karachi, Royal Book Company.
6. Chapra, M. Umer (2007), The Case Against Interest: Is It Compelling? Thunderbird International Business Review, Vol. 49 (2), March-April 2007, pp. 161-186.
7. Mohammad Nejatullah Siddiqi (2004), Riba, Bank Interest and the Rationale of Its Prohibition, Islamic Research and Training Institute.
8. Chapra, M. Umer (2000), Is it necessary to have Islamic Economics? Journal of Socio-Economics, 29, pp. 21-37.
9. Siddiqui, S.A., Understanding and Eliminating Riba: Can Islamic Financial Instrument is Meaningfully Implemented? Journal of Management and Social Science, Vol. 1, No. 2, (Autumn 2005), pp. 187-203.
10. Howard Davies (2003), Speech Delivered on Regulation and Islamic Finance at the Conference on Islamic Banking and Finance, Bahrain.
11. OCC Interpretive Letter No. 806 (October 17, 1997), [1997-1998 Transfer Binder] Fed. Banking L. Rep. (CCH) 81-253 (Islamic Home Finance Leases); OCC Interpretive Letter No. 867 (June 1, 1999), [1999-2000 Transfer Binder] Fed. Banking L. Rep. (CCH) 81-361 (Murabaha Financing Products).

12. C. Baxter Jr., Executive Vice President and General Counsel, Federal Reserve Bank of New York speech at the Seminar on Legal issues in the Islamic Financial Services Industry held at Kuwait, March 2, 2005.
13. SHAPE Financial Corporation's Report on, SHAPE Profit Sharing Deposit Products Fatwa.
14. Swee Keat, at The International Islamic Finance Forum Asia in Swiss hotel Merchant Court, Singapore 2006; Faizal Salieh (2006), Sri Lanka and the Scope for Islamic Banking, 'Islamic Finance News Guide', pp. 48-50; Bankers ask Government to allow Islamic Banks, 'The Hindu', September 6, 2007.

6

Summary and Conclusion

6.1 Summary

Bank is an essential component of the present world—individuals as well as public and private institutions can hardly operate without the institution of banking. Commercial banking as we find it today evolved over time and has become a stable institution, with principles and procedures that are well understood, accepted and practiced throughout the world. Modern banking operations are primarily based on interest. Banks receive money on interest and lend money on interest. This is prohibited in Islam. Since interest permeates all the operations of the banking system, the whole banking system is repugnant to the Muslims. However, in this fast moving world, more than 1400 years after the Prophet, can Muslims find room for the principles of their religion?

The answer comes with the fact that a global network of interest-free banks popularly known as Islamic banks has started to take shape based on the principles of Islamic finance laid down in the *Qur'an* and the Prophet's traditions 14 centuries ago. Islamic banking, based on the *Qur'anic* prohibition of charging interest, has moved from a theoretical concept to embrace more than 300 Islamic banks worldwide with a market capitalisation in excess of US$ 13 billion. Assets of Islamic banks worldwide are estimated at more than US$ 265 billion and financial investments above US$ 400 billion. Islamic bank deposits are estimated at over US$ 202 billion worldwide with average growth between 10 and 20 percent.

An Islamic bank is a financial institution that operates with the objective to implement and materialize the economic and financial principles of Islam in the banking arena. It is defined as "a financial and social institution whose objectives and operations as well as principles and practices must conform to the principles of *Islamic Shari'ah* (Jurisprudence), and which must avoid interest in any of its operations" and "a company which carries on Islamic banking business. Islamic banking business means banking business whose aims and operations do not involve any element which is not approved by the religion Islam."

It follows, therefore, that what makes Islamic banking different from conventional western banking is that there can be no interest (*Riba*) paid or charged for any transaction or service to ensure justice, welfare and non-exploitation.

Of course, the investments of an Islamic bank must be channelled to the *Islamic Shari'ah* approved sectors by Islamic modes of finance like *Mudaraba, Musharaka, Murabahah, Bai-Muajjal, Bai-Salam, Ijara, Hire Purchase,* etc., which are based on the sharing of risk and profit. Islamic bankers in effect generate "profit and loss" transactions in which the lender or bank shares in gains or losses based on the economic viability of the project and the credit worthiness of the customer.

This pattern of growth has attracted traditional banks such as Citibank, Kleinwort Benson, Midland Montagu, ANZ Grindlays and Goldman Sachs to look more closely for joint ventures with their Islamic counterparts for major financial transactions that accord with the *Shari'ah*. BNP Paribas has expanded its operations in Islamic finance and place it at the centre of the French bank's Middle East retail strategy. Deutsche Bank, Germany's biggest bank, is also planning to expand in producing services and products aimed at Muslim clients. In 2003, HSBC banking group became the first high street bank in Britain to offer mortgages and current accounts in accordance with *Shari'ah*. Customer service extends beyond spot transaction. It is much more than effectively meeting the customer needs or handling of their grievances. Customer service would be better if employees develop the desired attitude and motivations and develop their capabilities in the direction of effective customer service. Customer service is in fact the perception of a customer of the services he gets from his bank.

The human perception changes from individual to individual and within an individual from time to time. This change in perception of a customer of the service he gets makes the job of satisfying him at all point of time more challenging. It is, therefore, necessary for banks to continuously assess and reassess how customers perceive the services, what are the new and emerging customer expectations and how they can be satisfied on an ongoing basis. "Customer service is not merely the fulfilment of Government's guidelines or mechanical adherence to the time frames of services. It is a philosophy, an attitude of professional commitment which believes in the ultimate satisfaction of a customer's want."

The major element of service that a bank can offer to customer is the feeling that he/she is not just another number in computer, but a person in whom the bank takes a personal interest and with whom he/she can interface when problems arise. The computer and modern methods of analysis can be helpful in this regard. But in communicating the results, a little bit of human touch is essential. Furthermore, the frustration caused by impersonal services will allow the bank to give it a human face. 'Customer satisfaction,' through face to face interactions, looks for ways to make customers feel special. This special feeling is created through pleasant surprises; unique action or qualitative approach to service.

The essence of service excellence concentrates on listening, empowerment, innovation and making customers and employees part of the action. Service excellence focuses on making the service, the products and the surrounding more convenient, easier, neater and unique. Service excellence builds on excitement, relationships and trust. While a quality service approach uses some of these elements, they form the heart of service excellence. The service organizations, like banks play an important role in marketing various banking services to customer. Banks, basically work on the goodwill of the customers. The best way of servicing and prospering in the competitive environment is through providing prompt, relevant and efficient customer service at reasonable cost.

The successful organization is more effective at understanding the customers and winning new ones. Customer care is something a customer is entitled to. It is now widely recognized that if the customer is dissatisfied, the organization has no business to exist. Further, studies have revealed that it is cheaper to retain the existing customer than seeking a new one. It is also true that it is very challenging to retain the existing customer than to secure a new one.

Quality is a subject that can be viewed from many different angles. Above all, it is a guideline for providing high-level services. By searching for the key elements in the term quality, one should upgrade the level of his services. "Quality can be defined quite simply as the degree in which the expectation of customers is met with regards to a service offered." Quality is subjective. Quality in service industries has evolved into two distinct but related fields.

The first is service quality and the second is service excellence. These two fields are related the way marketing is related to sales and the way accounting is related to finance. Just as sales improve with good marketing and finance becomes possible through accounting, customer satisfaction improves when excellence finds its roots in meeting customer needs. These two fields overlap in several areas including listening to the customer, handling complaints and maintaining friendly service. However, the way each field addresses business customer interactions is distinctly different.

Quality service means delivery of promise through the design and execution of repeatable actions. The key to achieving service quality is conforming to standards. Service excellence, on the other hand, address to the defects in the present structure. Banking organizations are essentially human enterprises and customer service has therefore, to be necessarily taken care of through the persons working in banks. This has to be done by ensuring that the employees acquire capabilities that contribute to effective customer service, develop the desired attitude towards customers and are motivated to serve the customer better.

Employees of banks should have clear knowledge of various schemes of the banks. They should be able to understand the customer's requirements and suggest schemes to meet the needs of the customer. Effective customer service has to be backed by prompt and speedy decision-making process. The concept of accountability has affected decision making and in turn the quality of service. As global competition in financial services intensifies, service quality is emerging as a new frontier of banking competition. One reason is the increasing difficulty of competing on the basis of product and price. Many financial products are essentially commodities whose feature can easily be copied, and reliance on price competition is an invitation to steadily declining profit margins.

Customer satisfaction is the key to secure his/her loyalty and generate superior long-term performance. Therefore, banking institutions need to be made more responsive to the needs of the public. In current context, customer care and customer concern have become much more important. Nonetheless, banking services, in general, have still a long way to go for earning respect and esteem from the customers and public in respect of the quality of services they are providing to them. The systems and procedures followed in this respect should keep pace with the changing environment and changing demands. The service quality in contrast, provides a sustainable source of competitive advantage.

Customers are willing to pay more for higher quality service and competitors are not likely to replicate service dimensions as readily as product features. The service quality challenge becomes even more compelling because of increased role of conventional banks offering Islamic banking services. As a result customers who have inclination to do business only with Islamic banks have more opportunity to experience superior service and to compare service levels in different banking institutions. In this trend of competition, banking customers may have a stronger incentive to switch institutions in order to satisfy their rising expectations for service and value. The very nature of service marketing requires that service organizations should devote more attention on offering efficient services to the customers. As the services are invisible, they can gain confidence and goodwill only through efficient and prompt customer's services.

The Islamic Banks and Financial Institutions (IFIs) have become an integral part of the international finance and the regional bank industry. This study clearly shows the wide spread and growth of IFIs since 1970s. IFIs have developed from individual trials into an integrated industry with its own standard, criteria, products and institutions. The success of IFIs can be summarized as follows:

- Successes at the individual level including the high growth in attracting resources through investment and current accounts.
- Success at the corporate level is represented by the tendency of several commercial and industrial companies to take decisions at the board level to be financed according to *Shari'ah* compliant modes.
- Successes at the level of institutions offering Islamic banking and finance is reflected by the expansion of Islamic banking locally, regionally and internationally, a fact that makes conventional financial institutions display increased interest in delivering Islamic financial services with different structures and forms. Those institutions have not only established independent Islamic banks in terms of capital, financial statements and management, other local conventional banks have gone towards full conversion to Islamic banking in order to meet the market needs.

IFIs have been able to create a new type of investors with positive thoughts and rational investment decisions that lead them to play an active role in the economic and financial movement, instead of taking passive positions.

Banking is an activity where one is concerned with the management of other people's money. That is why bankers all over the world are conservative and cautious. Hence, the changes coming to the banking sector are usually slow. Furthermore, Islamic banking is just forty-three years old. It needs more time to mature and grow. Nevertheless, it may even be observed now that current scene of Islamic banking is dynamic in which changes within the system are continuously occurring. The need of the hour is to strengthen these emerging trends.

6.2 Suggestions for Improvement of Islamic Banks

1. The banks should implement well devised turnaround plan for strategic changes to grow new businesses and an aggressive loan recovery programme.
2. The banks should recapitalise and restructure balance sheet in a manner to address the issue of non-performing finances.
3. The banks' boards should revamp the IT infrastructure. It should approve a new IT blueprint for a bank-wide IT system. The system will be modular as well as scalable.
4. The banks should design a transformation programme to enhance their effectiveness and competitiveness. This programme should aim at the transformation of the organization and business operations.
5. The banks should establish a corporate investment banking division and beef up their treasury management and cash management divisions.
6. Cost rationalisation is always ongoing as part of the banks' goal to manage cost effectively. Towards this objective, several other initiatives should be implemented. For example, the outsourcing of non-critical operations, the

relocation of branches to more strategic locations and the disposal of non-core assets.

7. The banks should implement performance-linked reward programmes i.e., human capital development programme (HCDP) and structured training programmes (STPs). These programmes should be devised in a manner to attract and retain high quality talented staff which would ultimately result in the success of the banks. Banks should continue to make strategic changes necessary to take it to another level of growth and position it to compete with the best in the banking industry, locally and globally.

8. Banks should adapt and implement a refined service quality programme within a defined period of time

9. Banks should establish a quality leadership team (QLT) and stress on the importance of strong leadership, commitment, and support by top management to ensure the success of the quality effort.

- The primary role of QLT is to ensure that quality is integrated into management process and into provision products and services to customers.

- The QLT should ensure the development, maintenance of quality documentation and developing a quality performance indicators report.

- The QLT should ensure that the programs will lead to continuous improvement in terms of satisfaction, internal and external customers, performance, productivity and profitability.

- QLT should conduct self-assessment test and establish self-assessment committees or teams to compile and analyze it and develop strategies from the addressing results. Further, short- and long-term self-assessment improvement must be identified to be accomplished over years.

10. Banks should employ strategic quality services to the customers to improve their performance.

6.3 Suggestion for Establishment of Islamic Banking in India

The Indian Government should permit the establishment of Islamic banking in India on the following grounds:

1. Modern secular countries like Britain, United States, Singapore and Sri Lanka have successfully accommodated Islamic banking and Islamic banking products within their banking system. In Britain, the U.K. Financial Services has successfully resolved a number of regulatory issues including the problem of deposits in Islamic banks. This has enabled not only the setting up of Islamic Bank of Britain but also has enabled renowned banks to offer Islamic financial products. In United States of America, the flexible approach of the regulatory authorities has permitted two types of Islamic financing vehicles viz., *Ijara* and *Murabaha*. Singapore has been systematically reviewing its policies to ensure that Islamic finance is not disadvantaged vis-à-vis conventional finance. Singapore's existing regulatory framework with suitable refinements has facilitated the development of Islamic finance in Singapore. Where there are specific risks or impediments, rules have been refined to address these specific areas. It is to be specifically pointed out here that Islamic banks, *Takaful* and *retakaful* companies or Islamic capital markets players interested to operate in Singapore need not apply for a separate category of license; that is, the same licensing regime as that for conventional financial institutions will apply. Singapore has also amended its taxation laws to accommodate Islamic banks and Islamic financial products. Sri Lanka has also amended its Banking Act to accommodate Islamic banking. On the grounds of attracting capital as well as respecting the sentiments of the minorities Britain, United States, Britain, Singapore and Sri Lanka have facilitated Islamic banks and/or Islamic financial products.

2. The Indian banking sector has been opened considerably

in the past decade or so and openness to interest-free banks is a reasonable next step. Islamic banking is one way to better provide the disadvantaged Muslim minority (among others) with the tools it needs to improve its situation. The potential benefits of allowing Islamic banking include decreased economic disparity between the Muslim minority and the rest of the nation, better integration of that Muslim minority, and increased national economic growth. By creatively accommodating the ideological differences of its Muslim minority, and keeping an open mind about interest-free banking, India can position itself to reap these potential benefits. The Government of India can grow one step closer to actualizing the spirit of "garibi hatao" by reforming its banking sector and allowing the establishment of Islamic banks.

3. Launching Islamic banks in India has definite advantages. Firstly, providing acceptable bank mediated avenue of investment, savings of those who avoid interest based investments on religious grounds can be mobilised. Secondly, an increase in the number of financial products available in the market is good for all concerned. Thirdly, domestic interest free financial institutions will facilitate inflow of interest free foreign private investment. Lastly, it will allow reputed banks to market interest-free financial products, or even open 'Islamic Windows'.

6.4 Conclusion

Everyone realizes that Muslims need jobs, education and other support systems to develop just like any other citizen of the country. But it is ironic that in a secular country like India we need Islamic banking to promote Muslims lest they rot in poverty. It is strange but no poor Muslim in Bangladesh has accused Grameen Bank founder Mohammed Yunus of being a kafir for lending with interest. Moreover, there are provisions for interest-free banking even now. Banks can invest in zero-coupon bonds, short-term treasury bills and corporate bills—

all of which are based on implied interest rates, but do not actually pay interest. Any bank can offer you a portfolio account where your money is invested in non-interest-bearing securities. Individuals can open non-interest bearing current accounts. All of them in a sense comply with doctrine of Islamic banking. Islamic banking is not what is needed to help Muslims.

When below-poverty-line (BPL) families can be helped without communal identification and state benefits can be given on socio-economic grounds, why are Muslims being treated any differently? It is obvious that giving benefits on the basis of caste or religion is useful for political mobilization and hence is being pushed for politico-religious payoffs. Quotas, Islamic banking, and Sachar-induced victimhood are all one of a piece—they promote communal identity at the cost of true development. Those who support the plea for an alternate financing channel to support the Muslim community need to realize that India's banking is "inclusive" and the reluctance of some Muslims to use banks is a case of self-exclusion, not discrimination.

6.4.1 Future Outlook: There are many benefits to the development of interest-free banking finance in India which includes a potential bettering of the condition of India's largest minority, better integration of that minority into secular-democratic India, more savings across the country, an increase in the national GDP growth rate, beneficial for all entrepreneurs who have profitable proposals but lack collateral. Increased political involvement, decreased inequality, business ownership and wealth will all serve towards the growth of our economy. All Indians will benefit from the increase in the GDP, the decrease in welfare expenditure, an increase in tax revenues, creation of new savings, employment opportunities and mobilization of savings.

The benefits to India of promoting and opening itself to interest-free banking and finance are significant and numerous enough that the opportunity cannot be easily neglected. India's banking and financial sector should be reformed so as to allow and encourage Islamic banks to enter the market place. The dawn of an era of justice can, therefore, be visualised where the fruits of interest-free banking and finance system would be available to a large number of people leading to overall social and economic prosperity.

In this new environment, risk sharing will replace risk shifting and morality coupled with realism, will serve as the corrective to self-destructive outgrowth of current financial capitalism.

6.5 Suggestions for Further Research in Islamic Banking

The vast majority of the research relating to Islamic banking industry is related to its viability and financial aspects. Very little research has been made in the area of customer's needs, wants and the response of the Islamic banker. Banking industry is changing fast and Islamic banks should also match the changing environment. The following factors are believed to be responsible for the changing dynamics of the industry:

1. Changing client needs for financing and investment; cost reducing strategies and technologies.
2. Emerging new potential markets with different demographic and social characteristics; technology-based financial service products.
3. Regulatory reforms to align with financial modernization, In this environment, it is essential that further research should be carried out to study how quality relates to Islamic banking industry.

Further research should also develop models to determine where operating system breakdown occurs, why they occur and how they can be prevented.

Research should also be done to develop a benchmark which can be used to compare the performance of an Islamic bank with other banks' which adopt a quality programme.

Academic researchers can also use CARTER model to

build theories and new models which might be related to the issues of the Islamic banks' performance, environment and culture. In terms of implementation of SQ, research needs to be done to identify and eliminate the regulations, attitudes, policies, and so on, which may be an impediment to continued improvement. Within the limits of this research work, a glimpse of the issue and constraints in implementing Islamic banking in India has been highlighted.

However, further research can be pursued to study the banking laws of countries like Malaysia, Singapore, Sri Lanka, Bangladesh etc., which have permitted dual banking system. The role of central bank and their role in control of Islamic banks in mixed environment deserve more attention from researchers.

There is need for more empirical studies, particularly to evaluate the effectiveness of monetary policy and the tools for monetary management against the objectives and goals which have been set for them. Further, there is need for research to assess the impact of Islamic banking in mixed environment countries on macroeconomic magnitudes.

Bibliography

Bibliography

Abdullah, A. (1987), 'Islamic Banking', Journal of Islamic Banking and Finance, January-March, 4(1).

Abdeen, A.M. and Shook, D.N. (1984), The Saudi Financial System, J. Wiley and Sons, Chichester.

Abdel-Magib, M.F. (1981), 'Theory of Islamic Banks: Accounting Implications', International Journal of Accounting, Fall: 78-102.

Aftab, M. (1986), 'Pakistan Moves to Islamic Banking', The Banker, June: 57-60.

Ahmad, Ausaf (1987), Development and Problems of Islamic Banks, Islamic Research and Training Institute, IDB, Jeddah.

Ahmad, Norafifah and Sudin Haron (2002), 'Corporate Customer Perceptions of Islamic Banking Products and Services.' Proceedings of the Fifth Harvard University Forum on Islamic Finance, Cambridge, USA.

Ahmad, Sheikh Mahmud (1952), Economics of Islam, Lahore.

Ahmad, Ziauddin (1994), Islamic Banking: State of the Art, Islamic Research and Training Institute, IDB, Jeddah.

Akkas, Ali (1996), "Relative Efficiency of the Conventional and Islamic Banking System in Financing Investment"; Unpublished PhD. Dissertation, Dhaka University.

Al-Arabi, Mohammad Abdullah (1966), 'Contemporary Banking Transactions and Islam's Views Thereon', Islamic Review, London, May 1966: 10-16.

Ali, M. (ed.) (1982), Islamic Banks and Strategies of Economic Cooperation, New Century Publishers, London.

Al-Jarhi, Ma'bid Ali (1983), 'A Monetary and Financial Structure for an Interest-free Economy: Institutions, Mechanism and Policy', in Ziauddin, Ahmad et al. (eds.), Money and Banking in Islam, International Centre for Research in Islamic Economics, Jeddah, and Institute of Policy Studies, Islamabad.

Anas Zarqa, M. (1983), "An Islamic Perspective on the Economics of Discounting in Project Evaluation" in Ziauddin Ahmad et al. (eds.), Fiscal Policy and Resource Allocation in Islam, Arabia Monthly, April, No. 8.

Angur M., Nataraajan R. and Jahera J. (1999), "SQ in the Banking Industry: An Assessment in a Developing Economy", International Journal of Bank Marketing, 17(3).

Anthony T. and Addams, H. (2000), "SQ at Banks and Credit Unions", Managing SQ, 10(1).

Aravindan P and Punniyamoorty M. (2000), 'Service Quality Model to Measure Customer Satisfaction' in Ragavachari M. and Ramani K.V. (eds.) Delivering Service Quality, Macmillan India Ltd.

Arif Mohammad (1989), "Islamic Banking in Malaysia: Framework, Performance and Lessons", Journal of Islamic Economics, Vol. 2, No. 2.

Ariff, M. (1988), "Islamic Banking", Asian Pacific Economic Literature, 2-2.

Ariff, M. (l982), 'Monetary Policy in an Interest-free Islamic Economy: Nature and Scope' in M. Ariff, (ed.), Monetary and Fiscal Economics of Islam, International Centre for Research in Islamic Economics, Jeddah.

Avkiran N. (1994), 'Developing an Instrument to Measure Customer Service Quality in Branch Banking', International Journal of Bank Marketing; 12(6).

Bagsiraj, M.I. (2002), Islamic Financial Institutions of India: Progress, Problems and Prospects, Scientific Publishing Centre, King Abdul Aziz University.

Bank Islam Malaysia Berhad, Annual Report (2004), Kuala Lumpur.

'Bank Islam Malaysia Posts Profit in first Six Months of Financial Year' (2007), Annual Report of Bank Islam Malaysia.

Bank Muamalat Malaysia Berhad, Annual Report (2003), Kuala Lumpur.

Bank Negara Malaysia, (1994-2001), The Bank Negara Malaysia Quarterly Bulletin, Kuala Lumpur, Malaysia.

Bashir, A. (1999), 'Risk and Profitability Measures in Islamic Banks: The Case of Two Sudanese Banks', Islamic Economic Studies, Vol. 6, No. 2.

Berger, A. (1995), 'The Relationship between Capital and Earnings in Banking', Journal of Money, Credit and Banking Vol. 27.

Berry, L., Parasuraman, A. and Zeithaml, V. (1990), "Five Imperatives for Improving SQ", Sloan Management Review, Vol. 29, Summer.

Bitran, G. and Lojo, H. (1993), "A Framework for Analysing Service Operations", European Management Journal, 11(3).

Blanchard, R. and Galloway, R. (1994), 'Quality in Retail Banking', International Journal of Service Industry Management; 5(4).

Bolton, R. and Drew, J. (1991), 'A Multistage Model of Customers: Assessment of SQ and Value", Journal of Consumer Research, Vol. 17, March.

Boualem Bendjilali (1991), Book Review of Waqar Masood Khan, Towards an Interest-free Islamic Economic System" in Review of Islamic Economics, Vol. 1, No. 1.

Bourke, P. (1989), 'Concentration and Other Determinants of Bank Profitability in Europe, North America and Australia', Journal of Banking and Finance 13.

Bruce, N.C. (1986), 'Islamic Banking Moves East', Euromoney, July: 142-5.

Buttle, F. (1996), "SERVQUAL: Review, Critique, Research Agenda", European Journal of Marketing, 30(1).

Chapra Umer, M. (1985), Towards a Just Monetary System, Islamic Foundation, UK.

Chapra, M. Umer (2007), The Case Against Interest: Is It Compelling? Thunderbird International Business Review Vol. 49 (2), March-April.

Chapra, M. Umer (2000), Is it Necessary to have Islamic Economics? Journal of Socio-Economics, 29.

Choudhury, Masul Alam (1986), Contributions to Islamic Economic Theory: A Study in Social Economics, St. Martin Press, New York.

Contracts and Investment in an Interest Free Islamic Economy", International Monetary Fund Working Paper No. 86/12.

Council of Islamic Ideology, Pakistan (1981), Report on the Elimination of Interest from the Economy of Pakistan, Islamabad.

Council of Islamic Ideology, Pakistan (1981), The Elimination of Interest from the Economy of Pakistan, Council of Islamic Ideology, Islamabad.

Cronin, J. and Taylor, S. (1994), "SERVPERF versus SERVQUAL: Reconciling Performance-based and Perceptions-minus-expectations Measurement of SQ", Journal of Marketing, Vol. 58, January.

Demirguc-Kunt, A., and H. Huizinga (1997), 'Determinants of Commercial Bank Interest Margins and Profitability: Some International Evidence', Working Paper, Development Research Group, World Bank, Washington, D.C.

Dickey, D.A. and W.A. Fuller (1979), "Distribution of the Estimators for Autoregressive Time Series with a Unit Root" Journal of American Statistical Association, 74.

Dirrar, E. Elbeid (1996), "Economics and Financial Evaluation of Islamic Banking Operations: A Case of Bank Islam Malaysia 1983-1995", Unpublished paper, UIA.

Duri, A.A. (1986), "Baghdad", The Encyclopaedia of Islam, E.S. Brill, Leiden.

El-Asker, A.A.F. (1987), The Islamic Business Enterprise, Croom Helm, London.

El-Din, A.K. (1986), 'Ten Years of Islamic Banking', Journal of Islamic Banking and Finance, July-September, 3(3).

El-Gamal, Mahmoud Amin (2000), A Basic Guide to Contemporary Islamic Banking and Finance: Rice University, Houston.

Ennew, C., Reed, G. and Binks, M. (1993), 'Importance-Performance Analysis and the Measurement of SQ', European Journal of Marketing, 27(2).

Erol, C. and El-Bdour, R. (1989), 'Attitudes, Behaviour and Patronage Factors of Bank Customers towards Islamic Banks', International Journal of Banking Marketing, Vol. 7-6.

Fouad, Al-Omar (2000), 'Supervision, Regulation and Adaptation of Islamic Banks to the Best Standards: The Way Forward', paper presented to the Conference on Islamic Banking Supervision: AAOIFI, Bahrain, February.

Gafoor A.L.M. (1996), Interest-free Commercial Banking, ANS Noordeen, Kuala Lumpur.

Gerrad, P. and Cunningham, J. B. (1997), "Islamic Banking: A Study in Singapore", International Journal of Banking Marketing, Vol. 15-6.

Ghazali, A., et al. (eds.), An Introduction to Islamic Finance, Kuala Lumpur (Malaysia): Quill Publishers.

Goitein, S.D. (1967), A Mediterranean Society: University of California Press, Berkley and Los Angeles.

Granger, C.W.J. (1969), "Investigating Causal Relation by Econometric Models and Cross Spectral Methods," Econometrica, 37.

Gronroos, C. (1984), "A SQ Model and its Marketing Implications", European Journal of Marketing, Vol. 18.

Hadith compiled by Muslims (Kitab al-Musaqat).

Halim, Abdul (1986), 'Sources and Uses of Funds: A Study of Bank Islam Malaysia Berhad', paper presented to the Seminar on

Developing a System of Islamic Financial Instruments, organized by the Ministry of Finance Malaysia and the Islamic Development Bank, Kuala Lumpur.

Hamdi, Abdur Rahim (1992), Islamic Banking: Conceptual Framework and Practical Operations, Institute of Policy Studies, Islamabad.

Haq, Nadeem Ul, and Mirakhor, Abbas (1987), 'Saving Behaviour in an Economy without Fixed Interest', Theoretical Studies in Islamic Banking and Finance, Khan, Mohsin S. and Mirakhor, Abbas, (eds): The Institute for Research and Islamic Studies, Houston, Texas, United States.

Haque, Nadeem Ul and Mirakhor, Abbas (1986), 'Optimal Profit-Sharing', Princeton University Press, Princeton, NJ.

Haron and Planisek, L. (1994), 'Bank Patronage Factors of Muslim and Non-Muslim Customers', International Journal of Bank Marketing, Vol. 12 No. 1.

Haron, S., Ahmad, N., and Planisek, S. (1994), 'Bank Patronage Factors of Muslim and Non-Muslim Customers', International Journal of Bank Marketing, Vol. 12, No. 1.

Hassan, M. Kabir (1999), 'Islamic Banking in Theory and Practice: The Experience of Bangladesh', Managerial Finance, Vol. 25, and Vol. 5.

Hassan, M. Z. (2001), 'Challenges Towards Deepening of the Islamic Bond Market and Islamic Multi-Investment Funds', Paper presented at Kuala Lumpur International Summit of Islamic Banking and Finance, 19-21 February, Kuala Lumpur.

Hjarpe, Jan (1986), 'Mudaraba Banking and Takaful Insurance: The Question of Islamic Banks: Their Significance and Possible Impact', in Jan Selmer, and Loong Hoe Tan, Economic Relations between Scandinavia and ASEAN: Issues on Trade, Investment, Technology Transfer and Business Culture, University of Stockholm and Institute of South-east Asian Studies, Singapore.

Holy Qur'an Chapter 2, Verse 274.

Holy Qur'an Chapter 3, Verse 130.

Holy Qur'an Chapter 2, Verse 275, Chapter 2, Verse 278-281, Chapter 3, Verse 130, Chapter 4, Verse 160-161.

Holy Qur'an Chapter 9, Verse 60.

Homoud, S.H. (1985), Islamic Banking, Arabian Information, London.

Howard Davies (2003), Speech Delivered on Regulation and Islamic Finance at the Conference on Islamic Banking and Finance, Bahrain.

Huq, Azizul (l986), 'Utilization of Financial Investments: A Case Study of Bangladesh', paper submitted to the Seminar on Developing a System of Islamic Financial Instruments, organized by the Ministry of Finance Malaysia and the Islamic Development Bank, Kuala Lumpur.

IBCA (1997), BankScope Database, Bureau Van Dyck, New York, N.Y.

Ibrahim, Warde (2000), Islamic Finance in the Global Economy, University Press, Edinburgh.

IFC (1997), Emerging Market Database, Washington, D.C.

IMF (2000), International Financial Statistics Yearbook, Washington, D.C.

Institute of Islamic Banking and Insurance (1995), Encyclopaedia of Islamic Banking and Insurance, London: IIBI.

International Financial Crisis: From an Islamic Perspective (2009), Islamic Economic Research Centre, King Abdul Aziz University.

Iqbal, Z. and Mirakhor, Abbas (1987), Islamic Banking, International Monetary Fund, Occasional Paper 49, Washington D.C.

Iqbal, Zamir and Abbas Mirakhor (1999), 'Progress and Challenges of Islamic Banking', Thunderbird International Business Review, Vol. 41, No. 4/5.

Irshad S.A (1964), Interest-free Banking, Orient Press of Pakistan, Karachi.

Islamic Finance Directory, (2004), General Council for Islamic Banks and Financial Institutions, Manama.

Islamic Finance Directory, (2004), General Council for Islamic Banks and Financial Institutions, Manama.

Johnston, R. (1995), 'Determinants of SQ: Satisfiers and Dissatisfiers', International Journal of Service Industry Management, 6 (5).

Johnston, R. (1997), 'Identifying the Critical Determinants of SQ in Retail Banking: Importance and Effect", International Journal of Bank Marketing, 15(4).

Kahf, Monzer (1994), 'The Value of Money and Discounting in Islamic Perspective Re-visited', Review of Islamic Economics, Vol. 3 No. 2.

Kamila, B. and Nantel, J. (2000), 'A Reliable and Valid Measurement Scale for the Perceived Service Quality of Banks', International Journal of Bank Marketing, 18(2).

Karsten, I. (1982), 'Islam and Financial Intermediation', IMF Staff Papers, March, 29(1).

Khaf, Monzer and Khan, Tariqullah (1992), Principles of Islamic Financing (A Survey): Islamic Research and Training Institute, IDB, Jeddah.

Khan, Abdul Jabbar (1986), 'Non-interest Banking in Pakistan: A Case Study', paper presented to the Seminar on Developing a System of Islamic Financial Instruments, organized by the Ministry of Finance Malaysia and the Islamic Development Bank, Kuala Lumpur.

Khan, M.F. (1983), 'Profit and Loss Sharing: An Economic Analysis of an Islamic Financial System", Unpublished Ph.D. Dissertation, University Of Michigan.

Khan, M.S. (1986), 'Islamic Interest-free Banking', IMF Staff Papers, March, 33(1).

Khan, Mohsin S. and Abbas Mirakhor (1987) (eds.), Theoretical Studies in Islamic Banking and Finance: Institute for Research and Islamic Studies, Houston.

Khan, Muhammad Akram (1968), 'Theory of Employment in Islam', Islamic Literature, Karachi, XIV (4): 5-16.

Khan, W.M. (1985), 'Towards an Interest-Free Islamic Economic System', The Islamic Foundation, Leicester.

Lassar, W., Manolis, C. and Winsor, R. (2000), 'SQ Perspectives and Satisfaction in Private Banking', The International Journal of Bank Marketing, 18(4).

Le Blanc G. and Nguyen N. (1988), Customers' Perceptions of Service Quality in Financial Institutions, International Journal of Bank Marketing, 6(4).

Lewis, B., Orledge, J. and Mitchell, V. (1994), 'SQ: Students' Assessment of Banks and Building Societies', International Journal of Bank Marketing, 12(4).

Mabid Ali Al-Jarhi and Munawar, Iqbal (2001), 'Islamic Banking: Answers to Some Frequently Asked Questions', Occasional Paper 4, Islamic Research and Training Institute, Jeddah.

Man, Z. (1988), 'Islamic Banking: The Malaysian Experiences', Islamic Banking in South East Asia, Institute of South East Asian Studies, Singapore.

Mannan, M.A. (1970), Islamic Economics, Lahore.

Mersha T. and Adlakha V. (1992), 'Attributes of SQ: The Consumers' Perspective', International Journal of Service Industry Management, 3(3).

Metawa, S.A. and Almossawi, M. (1997), 'Banking Behavior of Islamic Bank Customers: Perspectives and Implications' International Journal of Bank Marketing, Vol. 16, No. 1.

Mirakhor, Abbas (1986), 'Some Theoretical Aspects of an Islamic Financial System', paper presented at a Conference on Islamic Banking sponsored by the Central Bank of the Islamic Republic of Iran, Tehran, 11-14 June.

Mohammad Abdullah, Al-Arabi (1966), 'Contemporary Banking Transactions and Islam's Views There On', Islamic Review, London, May.

Mohsin Khan (1987), 'Principles of Islamic Monetary Theory and Policy, Paper Presented at Seminar on Islamic Economics for University Teachers, Islamabad Pakistan.

Mohsin, M. (1982), 'Profile of Riba-free Banking', in M. Ariff (ed.), Naqvi, S.N.H., (1981) Ethics and Economics: An Islamic Synthesis, The Islamic Foundation, Leicester.

Molyneux, P., and J. Thornton (1992), 'Determinants of European Bank Profitability: A Note', Journal of Banking and Finance, 16.

Monzer, Kahf (1999), Islamic Banks at the Threshold of Third Millennium, Thunderbird International Business Review, Volume 41, Issue 4-5.

Monzer, Kahf, Clement M. Henry and Rodney Wilson (ed.) (2004), The Politics of Islamic Finance, Edinburgh University Press, France.

Naqvi, S.N.H. (1978), Ethical Foundations of Islamic Economics, Journal of Islamic Economics, Journal of Islamic Studies, Summer.

Naughton, S.A.J. and Tahir, M.A. (1988), 'Islamic Banking and Financial Development', Journal of Islamic Banking and Finance, 5 (2).

New Horizon (1996), 'News Monitor: Malaysia to Establish Islamic Index', New Horizon 52.

Nienhaus, V. (1983), 'Profitability of Islamic PLS Banks Competing with Interest Banks: Problems and Prospects', Journal of Research in Islamic Economics, 1 (1).

Nien-haus, V. (1988), 'Profitability of Islamic PLS Banks Competing with Interest Banks: Problems and Prospects', Journal of Research in Islamic Economics, 1(1).

Noraffifah, A. (2000), 'The Effects of Conventional Interest Rates and Rate of Profit on Funds Deposited With Islamic Banking System in Malaysia', International Journal of Islamic Financial Services, 1, No. 3.

Obaidullah, Mohammed (2005), Islamic Financial Services, King Abdul Aziz University, Islamic Economics Research Centre, Jeddah.

OCC Interpretive Letter No. 806 (October 17, 1997), [1997-1998 Transfer Binder] Fed. Banking L. Rep. (CCH) 81-253 (Islamic Home Finance Leases); OCC Interpretive Letter No. 867 (June 1, 1999), [1999-2000 Transfer Binder] Fed. Banking L. Rep. (CCH) 81-361 (Murabaha Financing Products).

Oliver, R.L. (1993), 'A Conceptual Model of SQ and Service Satisfaction: Compatible Goals, Different Concepts', Advances in Services Marketing and Management, Vol. 2, JAI Press, Greenwich, CT.

Paper submitted on the Occasion of The International Islamic Finance Forum held on 26-29 September 2005, Istanbul Turkey.

Partadireja, Ace (1974), 'Rural Credit: The Ijon System', Bulletin of Indonesian Economic Studies, 10 (3).

Patterson, P.G. and L. Johnson (1993), 'Disconfirmation of Expectations and Gap Model of Service Quality: An Integrated Paradigm', Journal of Consumer Satisfaction, Dissatisfaction and Complaint Behaviour, Vol. 6.

Perry F.E. (1979), 'Dictionary of Banking', Mcdonald and Evans, pp. 61-62; Spreng, R.G., Harrell and Mackoy, (1995), 'Service Recovery: Impact on Satisfaction and Intentions', Journal of Service Marketing, Vol. 9, No. 1.

Qureshi, Anvar Iqbal (1946), Islam and Theory of Interest, Sh. M. Asraf, Lahore.

Rad, Tourani A. (1991), 'Theoretical and Practical Aspects of the Interest-free Banking System', Netherlands Institute voor her Bank-en Effectenbedrijf, Amsterdam.

Radiah A.K. (1993), 'Performance and Market Implication of Islamic Banking (A Case Study of Bank Islam Malaysia Berhad)', Unpublished Ph.D Thesis.

Rahman, Fazalur, 'Riba and Interest', Islamic Studies, Karachi, 3(l): 1-43.

Ready, R.K. (1981), 'The March Toward Self-determination', Paper presented at the First Advanced Course on Islamic Banks, International Institute of Islamic Banking and Economics, Cairo, 28 August-17 September.

Report of Malaysia's Central Bank, Bank Negara Malaysia (2007) on Islamic Banking in Malaysia.

Rosa, D.A. (1986), 'Islamic Financial Policies and Domestic Resource Mobilisation', Savings and Development, 2.

Royne, M. (1996), 'Demographic Discriminators of SQ in the Banking Industry', The Journal of Services Marketing, 10(4).

Salama, Abidin Ahmad (1986), 'Utilisation of Financial Instruments: A Case Study of Faisal Islamic Bank (Sudan)', Paper submitted to the Seminar on Developing a System of Islamic Financial Instruments, organized by the Ministry of Finance Malaysia and the Islamic Development Bank, Kuala Lumpur.

Samuel, K. (1999), 'Change for the Better via ISO 9000 and TQM', Management Decision, 37(4).

Scharf, T.W. (1983), Arab and Islamic Banks, OECD, Paris.

Shanmugam, B. (1995), 'The Effects of Rates of Profit on Islamic Bank's Deposits: A Note', Journal of Islamic Banking and Finance, 12, No. 2.

Sheikh, Mahmud Ahmad (1952), Economics of Islam, Lahore, Ch. V11.

Siddiqi, M. Nejatullah (1967), Banking Without Interest (Urdu), Lahore: Islamic Publications, Revised Version (1983).

Siddiqi, Nejatullah M. (1983), Banking Without Interest, Islamic Foundation, UK.

Siddiqi, Nejatullah M. (1980, 1981), Muslim Economic Thinking: A Survey of Contemporary Literature in Studies in Islamic Economics, (eds.) Kurshid Ahmed, Islamic Foundation, Leicester.

Siddiqi, Nejatullah M., 'Islamic Banking: Theory and Practice' in M. Ariff (1988) (ed.), Islamic Banking in South East Asia, Asian Pacific Economic Literature, Vol. 2, No. 2.

Siddiqui, S.A. (2005), Understanding and Eliminating Riba: Can Islamic Financial Instrument is Meaningfully Implemented? Journal of Management and Social Science, Vol. 1, No. 2, Autumn.

Stafford, M. (1996), 'Demographic Discriminators of SQ in the Banking Industry', Journal of Services Marketing, 10(4).

Surah al-Rum (Chapter 30), verse 39; Surah al-Nisa (Chapter 39), verse 161; Surah al-Imran (Chapter 3), verses 130-2; Surah al-Baqarah (Chapter 2), verses 275-281; See Yusuf Ali's Translation of the *Qur'an*.

Su'ud, M. Abu, n.d. 'The Economic Order Within the General Conception of the Islamic Way of Life', Islamic Review, London, 55 (2) and (3): 11-l4.

The World Bank Economic Review, Vol. 10, No. 2.

Thomas C. Baxter Jr., (2005), Executive Vice President and General Counsel, Federal Reserve Bank of New York speech at the Seminar on Legal issues in the Islamic Financial Services Industry held at Kuwait, March 2.

Udovitch, Abraham L. (1970), Partnership and Profit in Medieval Islam, Princeton University Press, Princeton, N.J.

Umer, Chapra M. (1982), 'Money and Banking in an Islamic Economy' in M. Ariff (ed.), 'Monetary Policy and Fiscal Economics of Islam, International centre for Research in Islamic Economics, Jeddah.

Usmani, Taqi Muhammed (1998), 'An Introduction to Islamic Finance', Idara Isha'at e Diniyat, New Delhi, p. 47.

Uzair, Mohamed (1978), Interest-free Banking, Royal Book Co., Karachi, Pakistan.

Uzair, Mohammad (l955), An Outline of Interest-less Banking, Raihan Publications, Karachi.

Waqar Masood Khan (1985), Towards an Interest-free Islamic Economic System, Islamic Foundation, UK.

White, H. (1980), 'A Heteroskedasticity Consistent Covariance Matrix Estimator and a Direct Test for Heteroskedasticity', Econometrica, Vol. 48, No. 4.

Wilson, Rodney (ed.) (1990), Islamic Financial Markets, Routledge, London.

Yavas, U., Bilgin, Z. and Shemwell, D. (1997), 'SQ in the Banking Sector in an Emerging Economy: A Consumer Survey', International Journal of Bank Marketing, 15(6).

Zaidi, N.A. (l987), 'Profit Rates Policy for PLS Depositors', Journal of Islamic Banking and Finance, 4 (4).

Zakariya, Man (1988), 'Islamic Banking: The Malaysian Experience', in Arif, Islamic Banking, Asian Pacific Economic Literature, Vol. 2, No. 2.

Zamir, Iqbal and Abbas Mirakhor (1987), Islamic Banking,

International Monetary Fund Occasional Paper 49, Washington D.C.

Zarqa, Anas M. (1983), 'Stability in an Interest-free Islamic Economy: A Note', Pakistan Journal of Applied Economics, Winter.

Index

Index